*Ice With
Everything*

H. W. TILMAN

Ice With Everything

GRAY

Gray's Publishing Ltd., Sidney, British Columbia, Canada

ISBN 0-88826-050-4

Published simultaneously in the United Kingdom by
NAUTICAL PUBLISHING COMPANY LIMITED

Printed and bound in Canada by
EVERGREEN PRESS LIMITED
Vancouver, British Columbia

Contents

Plates

MAPS

To the Faeroes

For most men, as Epicurus has remarked, rest is stagnation and activity madness. Mad or not, the activity that I have been pursuing for the last twenty years takes the form of voyages to remote, mountainous regions. In more recent years this has invariably meant a summer voyage to the Arctic, either to the west or east coast of Greenland. By now such voyages have become a habit, and a worse habit is that of writing about them. In these pages are descriptions of the three most recent voyages, those of 1971, 1972 and 1973, the first comparatively humdrum, the second totally disastrous, and the third exceedingly troublesome.

Upon her return from the 1970 voyage to south-west Greenland *Seabreeze* had been hauled out in order that the hull could be examined. The ice she had encountered, besides inflicting some deep scars, had started one or two planks, yet considering that throughout the two months spent upon the coast she had never been out of sight of ice and had spent five days in the pack moored to a floe, she had got off lightly. The defects having been put right, she received her annual coat of anti-fouling and went back into the water for the winter. *Seabreeze*, by the way, is a Bristol Channel pilot cutter built in 1899, length 49 ft., beam 14 ft. 4 in., drawing 7 ft. 6 in., and of about 33 tons T.M. A boat built in 1899 may seem on the old side for such voyages, but I have a liking for craft of traditional lines and rig and a foolish liking for doing things the hard way, for apart from her engine *Seabreeze* is much as she was when a working boat. Nothing, of course, could be more untraditional than an engine, but to be without one on the Greenland coast is a grievous handicap. Apart from ice or skerries upon which a sailing vessel becalmed might drift helplessly, there is the matter of making progress. In the fjords winds are light and fitful so that without an engine one might spend days drifting about unable to reach one's goal or even to reach an anchorage. Pilot cutters are necessarily old, for none were built after about 1910, but they are eminently suitable for these voyages—ample stowage space, sturdily built, and able sea-boats—qualities that had been impressed upon me in the years from 1954 to 1968 when I had been the happy owner of *Mischief*, a pilot cutter built in 1906.

Barmouth, where I live, is 230 miles from Lymington where *Seabreeze* lay. Why not, one might think, move the boat to Wales or oneself to Hampshire? Long use and wont and the inability to get out of a rut together make one reason and besides that there is the absence of hills in Hampshire and the scarcity of boatyards in Wales. In winter a boat out of commission is a forlorn habitation and on my periodical visits I used to put up at a guest-house. When this closed I had perforce to sleep on board, a salutary exercise that brought home to one the dangers that beset a boat laid up for the winter. "Death and decay in all around I see" would be a mild description. From stem to stern the deckhead dripped moisture, mildew bloomed on the varnish, and one half expected to find toadstools sprouting in the lockers. In the dark and more inaccessible corners that are features of old boats, they probably did. *Seabreeze*, I believed, would last my time, but not unless steps were taken to combat damp and decay during the winter lay-up. A big canvas cover supported on booms over the whole length of the boat not only kept the rain off the deck but allowed all hatches and skylights to be left wide open. This made a big difference and since on these visits I had a stove going non-stop the cabin soon became less like the family vault.

Northern waters offer a wide choice of places that are accessible to a small boat in summer—Spitsbergen, Jan Mayen, Baffin Island, and both the coasts of Greenland. Including fjords, some of which are a hundred miles long, Greenland has a coast line of some 20,000 miles, hence inexhaustible riches for anyone who has at command his own transport in the form of an able boat. One is often asked what is the attraction of Greenland and the reply would be, where else would a man who desires both the hills and the sea want to go. Where, within a month's sail from home, he can see mountains that are Alpine both in character and stature and glaciers vastly in excess of Alpine stature; where there are numerous uninhabited, little-known fjords; a coast fringed with islands, islets, and skerries equally devoid of human life; where a man in his own boat, though hardly to be called an explorer, even at this late date can, in Belloc's words, "feel as felt the earlier man in a happier time, and see the world as they saw it". Added to that are the icebergs of all shapes and sizes, their massive grandeur all the more impressive when seen at close quarters from the deck of a small boat; finally, and best of all, the austere beauty of a summer's day off the Greenland coast, sea, snow mountains, and ice, and overhead the pale northern sky.

Wide though the choice of objectives in northern waters may be, I had no doubts about where we ought to make for in 1971. No one likes being defeated and our tame acceptance of defeat when trying to reach Scoresby Sound in 1969 still rankled. On that occasion, when some 20 miles south of C. Brewster, the southern entrance to the Sound, what I called a polite mutiny on the part of the crew had obliged us to give up and return prematurely home. Admittedly, our five days of groping in continuous fog had not been encouraging and when the fog had cleared sufficiently to reveal a lot of ice—a phenomenon not unexpected in the Arctic— the crew decided they had seen enough. Ice reports that I obtained after our return showed that we might have had trouble in enter- ing the Sound and certainly more when leaving it, but this is what the voyager likes to discover for himself and this is what a voyage of this kind is all about.

Scoresby Sound is in Lat. 70° N. on the east coast of Greenland. The Sound was named after his father by William Scoresby, who in 1882 surveyed and charted some 400 miles of the east coast. Like his father, he was one of the most successful whaling captains sailing out of Whitby and, not content with this, he went on to become an explorer, a scientist, a Fellow of the Royal Society, and at last a parson. Having made his first voyage with his father at the age of eleven, after twenty-five years at sea he went to Cam- bridge to take a degree and entered the Church. His two-volume book *An Account of the Arctic Regions*, with a history and descrip- tion of the northern whale-fishery, should be read if only for the story of how they saved the whaler *Elsie*, nipped and badly holed a hundred miles inside the pack.

The earlier statement that the east coast of Greenland is acces- sible in summer to a small boat needs qualifying. South of Ang- magssalik (Lat. 66° N.) the coast is usually fairly free of ice by the end of July, while north of that it seldom is. Ice conditions vary a lot from year to year but in most years there is little chance of finding Scoresby Sound open before the beginning of August. The *Arctic Pilot* has this to say:

> Conditions are very variable. The ice in the Sound generally breaks up about the middle of July. Navigation is usually possible in August and September and frequently also in the latter part of July. Navigation after mid-September may be risky owing to the onset of gales. The approaches to Scoresby Sound are more likely to be free from ice in late September than at any other time but in severe ice years they may not uncover at all.

Navigable in this context means for moderate-sized steamers or small sealers built to withstand ice. Obviously for an unstrengthened boat such as *Seabreeze* conditions need to be unusually good. It is a matter of luck. Ice conditions cannot be foreseen or predicted and even ice reports received a few days beforehand are of little value since, by the time one gets there, the situation may have entirely altered. The only way is to go there and see, and in the case of Scoresby Sound, by the time this has been done, say in mid-August, supposing one is repulsed, there is no time left for anything but to go home. A target like this, more likely to be missed than hit, is not to be aimed at too frequently. In 1970, for instance, I gave up Scoresby Sound in favour of West Greenland because I had in the crew two Australian climbers who had come all that way in the hope of climbing a Greenland mountain and I could not afford to disappoint them by attempting Scoresby Sound and failing. Moreover, for climbing purposes, reaching the Sound, though meritorious, is not enough. The real objective is two little-known, highly mountainous islands on which no climbing, I believe has yet been done, and these lie some 70 miles inside the entrance. Seventy miles is no small distance and since the Sound would be by no means entirely ice-free it would probably have to be done under the engine. There are therefore difficulties and hazards enough in the way of winning this particular prize. Scoresby Sound, by the way, is the largest fjord in the world. Some merit would be acquired by getting there in a small boat and at the back of it are these two islands studded with unclimbed peaks.

Provided with an able boat and a highly desirable objective there remained only the matter of crew, a crew that must not include any "pikers", as my Australian and New Zealand friends call them, those whose hearts are not in it and who are ready to quit at the first sign of trouble. I already had one man who could be relied upon in Bob Comlay; he sailed with us in 1970 and wished to do so again. Once is not always enough, as some might think would be the case with these voyages. Several have made two voyages, while one, Charles Marriott, even more eccentric, has made four. I had equal confidence, too, in another candidate, though I had not yet met him. He had been recommended to me by Phil Temple who had been on the Heard Island voyage, and I had therefore no hesitation about taking Max Smart, a New Zealander living in England. While on a visit to Snowdonia he came over to Bodowen to see me. Hairy as a prophet and strong as a horse, he lent an energetic and powerful hand clearing some of our local jungle. On *Seabreeze* there are no winches to assist in setting up halyards and sheets, nor are they needed, provided one has a Max Smart or someone as strong on board.

For a cook I had to advertise as I had done for the previous voyage and for several others before that. The market for this commodity, "cook for a cool voyage" as I put it, seemed to be barely steady, the number of replies received being down on that of the previous year. Of the ten who replied most were for various reasons self-cancelling and all but one of the few left in the running either disliked the tone of my letters or had second and better thoughts. A line I remember from some children's book ran, "Little Hippo, bound to win, was the only one left in", and on this occasion the only one left in was Marius Dakin, an art student, or rather hoping to qualify as an art student in the coming autumn. He had no sea experience but he could cook and what is more he enjoyed cooking. He was something of an expert photographer and for this trip hoped to borrow father's expensive camera, father being a professional. Wise in his generation, father thought differently. So instead Marius undertook to make a film using the second-hand 16 mm. camera that I had bought for the southern voyage of 1966–67. Like the other films taken on past voyages, and indeed like many that are inflicted on the public, the result hardly justified the expense.

The name of the man whom I had secured for fourth place

escapes me, as he himself escaped by dropping out at the last moment. By then we were fitting out and it seemed as if only a miracle could save us from sailing short-handed. Though three watch-keepers could manage well enough, it would be uncommonly hard work on a four-month voyage. In their working days pilot cutters were sailed by two men or even a man and an apprentice, but they would be out for a few days or a week at most and they were real sailors. The unexpected happened. I had a letter from one Peter Marsh who had done a lot of week-end sailing and had built for himself a catamaran in which he proposed sailing to Iceland. He wrote mainly to ask for advice but also implied that he would like to gain some first-hand experience in northern waters. "When they bring you a heifer be ready with the rope", as they say in Spain. I sent him a telegram, he arrived at Lymington on 29th May, and the crew was complete.

Max arrived next day humping a vast load, and then Marius, in pink bell-bottom trousers and green velvet jacket, with a guitar slung behind, looking more like a troubadour than a sea-cook. Bob Comlay, a student at Bangor University, had examinations to take and would not join until sailing day, which was to be 12th June. Marius, the aesthete, shocked by the décor of the galley, got to work on it. Nominally the galley is painted white, until after five months with three Primus stoves in action it assumes a darker hue, pale yellow in the outer parts, becoming dark brown towards the centre, and finally jet black immediately above the stoves. Having stripped off the mixture of paint and carbon—no light task—Marius painted the bulkhead eggshell blue, picked out the beams in black, and the deckhead between in white, and very smart it looked.

With the weather remaining on the whole unfavourable and only three hands available we needed all the time allowed for fitting out. Art is long and time is fleeting, I thought, as I watched Marius so preoccupied with painting the galley that he had no time for anything else. In a ketch lying outside *Seabreeze* were a Mr. and Mrs. Habens who were always ready with advice and assistance, urgently needed when it came to the tricky manœuvre of moving *Seabreeze* to the outside berth and turning her head in the right direction for off. Sorting out the bow lines, breast lines, stern lines, and springs by which the boats were moored might have baffled a professional dock-master.

1. The river on Upernivik.   *Photo: Ilan Rosengarten*

2. "Picturesque" Greenland bergs seen over the boom of *Sea Breeze* in Denmark Strait. These are more buoyant than the block bergs with precipitous sides, but still have three times as much ice submerged as shows above the water.

With the arrival of Bob Comlay on 12th June we were ready to go. For some days I had been dithering over the question of whether to sail east or west-about, up Channel or down, and had still only reached the infirm decision of waiting to see what the weather might be when we were outside the Needles. We were bound first for the Faeroes, a convenient stopping place on the way to Iceland, and thence to east Greenland. By way of the North Sea it is possibly 100 miles shorter than by the Irish Sea and the Minches, a difference too slight to be of much account to a sailing vessel where the length of a passage is reckoned in the number of days it takes rather than the distance between ports. Calculations as to the length of the rhumb line course are of little use since the distance that will have to be sailed depends upon the winds encountered. If foul winds prevail one might sail many miles and still make no progress. The only real reason I had for going by way of the North Sea was that we had not been there before, while among several other reasons for not going that way was the density of steamer traffic in Dover Straits. Curiosity is said to betoken a generous mind and on this occasion curiosity prevailed. Meeting a westerly wind outside the Needles we turned eastwards and when it had taken us far enough in that direction to preclude any idea of our turning back the wind swung round to the east. So on the next day we found ourselves approaching the most congested shipping lanes in the world with a contrary wind and in thick weather.

The passage of the Straits proved less harrowing than I had anticipated, but it was luck rather than skill that brought us through. The thick weather prevented us from knowing where we were, a piece of knowledge that is particularly essential in a place like Dover Straits. Buoys abound, but the only one we passed we failed to identify, distracted perhaps by the German tanker that appeared out of the murk astern, hooting and going dead slow. Nor did we make rapid progress. On consecutive days, on different tacks, we twice sighted Dungeness to the north-east, until at last on the evening of 15th June a breeze at north-west sprang up to continue all night and all the next day, by which time we were clear of the Narrows and had the Galloper light-vessel abeam. Meantime all was not well with the unlucky Peter who had been seasick from the time we passed the Needles, gamely taking his trick at the helm with the appearance and alacrity of a corpse. He proved to be one of those rare cases of seasickness for whom time and wont is no cure, and the sailing that he had previously done, confined to week-ends, had not lasted long enough for him to discover this. He stuck it out until we reached Iceland when it had become abundantly clear that his sickness was chronic. Rather than face another two or three months' misery, during which time he would be little use on board, he rightly decided to quit.

For the whole of a sunny afternoon, with all sails down, we drifted quietly back to the Newark light-vessel which we had passed earlier in the day. Various jobs that needed doing to the mainsail could now be done, hauling out the peak and clew, tightening up the gaff lacing. On the shrouds *Seabreeze* had the appropriate lanyards of $1\frac{3}{4}$ in. tarred Italian hemp (not easily found nowadays) instead of rigging screws, and these had to be set up again until they were bar taut. These sort of "sailorising" jobs which are fun to do are neither needed nor known on modern yachts.

In the North Sea one expects to see oil rigs, just as in the Arctic one expects to see icebergs. Like bergs, these are not marked on the chart, at least not until oil or gas has been struck when the rig is likely to become a semi-permanent feature; so that when we sighted a cluster of lights where according to the chart no lights should have been it was not difficult to guess what they were. No doubt the positions of rigs not yet marked on the chart are notified in *Notices to Mariners*, the weekly publication to which amateur sailors like ourselves should pay more attention. When to the west of the British Isles and listening to the shipping forecast I always have the impression that the North Sea has more than a fair share of gales and have accordingly felt sorry for any yachtsmen there. Perhaps we were lucky. The only gale warning we had proved to be a false alarm. We made good progress and by dawn of 23rd June found ourselves off the entrance to Pentland Firth, so confused, I confess, by the profusion of lights in sight that it took me some time to grasp the fact. I had intended going by way of Fair Isle through the wide strait between the Shetlands and the Orkneys, but the settled weather combined, of course, with curiosity induced me to try the Pentland Firth. With the tide running the wrong way we foolishly tried bucking it, helped by a fresh south-easterly breeze and with the engine going, an impossible feat for *Seabreeze* even with a favourable gale. Off Duncansby

Head we started going rapidly backwards, so we ran off north-east towards the Skerries where we were chased in a frightening way by an advancing tide-rip. When the wind died the tide turned in our favour and by evening we were through the Firth and admiring the Old Man of Hoy all aglow in the setting sun. There were now only some 200 miles to go and two days later, thanks to fair winds we sighted the familiar Lille Dimon, the 1,200 ft. high rocky island, shaped like a haystack, an unmistakable mark when approaching the Faeroes from the south-east.

CHAPTER TWO

The Faeroes and Iceland

A freshening northerly wind and the onset of rain that evening
seemed to betoken a dirty night. Not liking the prospect of beating
north to Nolso fjord and Thorshavn, which was our destination, we
ran off west into Skuo fjord where, at its head, there was the sheltered
anchorage of Sands Vaag. The fjord did not provide the lee that
we had expected. Fierce gusts swept down from the cliffs of Sando
Island to the north, tearing the water white as they hit. The whole
mainsail when full of wind is hard to tame so we rolled in several
reefs in order to have things under control before reaching the
anchorage. By 6 p.m., when we anchored off the village, the wind
had risen to gale force, the rain streaming down. The anchorage
is sheltered from all but a south-east wind when it would become
untenable. We set an anchor watch.

The wind had eased by morning though still at north, and since
it was a thick, mizzling day we lay at earth, as Jorrocks would say.
There are some 600 people in Sands Vaag, a village remarkable
in that not only several of the houses but also the fairly large church
have roofs of turf. At this time of year the grass on the roofs was
long enough for hay-making; the roofs rippled in the wind and one
wondered whether they were ever scythed. The people live by
sheep-farming and inshore fishing from open boats of traditional
Norse lines.

It is strange that although the rise and fall of the tide at the
Faeroes is but a few feet, the tidal stream runs with great force
in the fjords and off the headlands. While carefully timing our
departure to catch the north-going stream I stupidly overlooked
the fact that the north-going stream would also be flooding into
Skuo fjord. The engine had to work hard until we reached the sea
where we hoisted sail and had the tide under us all the way to

Nolso fjord. Failure to keep charts and *Pilot* books bang up to date, as well as the neglecting of *Notices to Mariners*, is another fault of the amateur sailor, a fault that caused us some embarrassment off Thorshavn. Look where we might we could see no sign of the entrance marked by a beacon on the end of the breakwater. There seemed to be no end to the breakwater and consequently no entrance. To enquire is neither a disaster nor a disgrace so we hailed a youth cavorting about in a speed-boat. The breakwater was being extended, the beacon had been removed, and the new entrance temporarily marked by an inconspicuous buoy. All of which would no doubt have been noted on an up-to-date chart.

We picked up the same buoy that we had used on previous visits close to *Westward Ho*, a fine big ketch built at Hull in 1880. They were giving her a major refit and in consequence she looked a bit dishevelled. After rowing ashore and walking to the Customs Office I found when I got there that they had already been on board to seal our liquor store. Like Iceland, the Faeroes are nominally "dry". I had the impression that they had not been much taken by my hairy crew. Max who had started out hairy now looked like the Wild Man of Borneo himself, his eyes just discernable through a matted undergrowth of hair. He and Peter forthwith went ashore to stretch their legs on the hill behind the town where they bivouacked for the night. Though Max enjoyed life at sea his real love was for mountains, to climb them or to camp among them. Peter, half inclined to give up here, decided to wait and see how he fared on the next leg to Iceland.

Having taken on water at the fish-wharf we sailed on 30th June for Reykjavik going north-about round the top of the Faeroes. Next day as soon as we met a bit of wind and sea Peter succumbed, nor was Max quite himself, showing less than his usual interest in the pasta and duff that we had for supper—a little heavy on the carbohydrates, perhaps, but as the Chinese say, a well-filled stomach is the great thing, all else is luxury. One expects plenty of wind south-east of Iceland, the track followed by most of the depressions that cross the Atlantic. The harder blows seldom lasted long, which was just as well because we were short-handed. Owing to his inability to eat anything Peter was not up to doing much beyond his two-hour trick at the helm.

On 6th July, in thick drizzling weather, we were somewhere

south of the Vestmannaejar, a group of islands and rocks 20 miles south of the Iceland coast, noted for volcanic activity. Heimaey, the fishing port of the Vestmannaejar, had recently been overwhelmed by a volcanic eruption. Also in this group is Surtsey, the volcanic island which suddenly appeared on 14th November 1963. "Appeared" is hardly the word for its tumultuous birth, a birth attended by violent explosions hurling clouds of smoke, steam, ash, and pumice thousands of feet into the air. Only when the wind blew away some of this cloud could it be seen that a new island had emerged from the sea. *Notices to Mariners* of 3rd January 1964 had this warning note:

> A submarine volcanic eruption has formed an island about half a mile in diameter and 250 ft. high in position 63° 18′ N. 20° 36′ W. Eruption is continuing and mariners are warned to keep clear of the area.

That mariners had to wait so long for this news to be published may have been owing to the Christmas holidays, or more likely it was in the hope that the island might disappear almost as suddenly as it had appeared; for unless and until lava begins to flow the existence of such islands may be only ephemeral. By April 1964 the island had grown to nearly a mile in length and 500 ft. in height. The Icelanders called it Surtsey and the volcano, which was still active, was called Surtur after the Fire Giant of Norse mythology, who comes from the south when the world ends to burn up everything. On passage to Iceland in *Mischief* in June 1964 two of us had landed on Surtsey, complete with cine-camera, and climbed to the rim of the volcano. The crater into which we had peered belched merely smoke and fumes instead of the cauldron of molten, fiery lava that we had hopefully expected to see. The whole place smelt like a coke oven, and one sensed, too, that the thing was still alive and growing. Our visit had been well or ill timed according to the point of view. Lava had only begun flowing on 4th April when rivers overflowed the crater to pour down into the sea. At the end of April the flow ceased and did not begin again until 9th July, a fortnight after our visit.

On 15th July 1965, still in *Mischief*, we again visited the area, guided from 30 miles away by a vast column of smoke. This came from a new island that had just erupted about a mile away from Surtsey which by then lay dormant. We hove-to to watch.

The vast white column of smoke ascended continuously, while every few minutes a fresh explosion flung a jet-black cloud of smoke, ash, and lumps of pumice, hundreds of feet into the air. Away to leeward, below the white smoke, curtains of ash drifted down to the sea. For an hour we lay and watched this remarkable sight until at length the activity subsided.

Having thus a proprietary interest in Surtsey I much wished to see it again in 1971. In the thick prevailing weather, however, I doubted our finding it even had there been a column of smoke to guide us; but by luck we spotted a lone rock which from its shape I recognised as one of the Vestmannaejar lying close to Surtsey, and soon after a big island, which was undoubtedly Surtsey, came into view. It had grown considerably in six years and the small island that had been so violent in 1965 had linked up with its parent. Except for some slight smoke or steam from four widely separated fumaroles there was no hint of activity. Scientists of various 'ologies are keeping a close watch on Surtsey to see how nature starts work on virgin territory. In 1964 we had noticed only some beer bottles.

Two days later, helped by light westerly winds, we sailed up the 50-mile wide bight of Faxafloi and between the piers into Reykjavik harbour. While we were handing the sails and wondering where to find a berth we were hailed from the shore and directed to one of the many steamer wharves, at that moment vacant. Usually a yacht is ignored and left to find its own accommodation from whence in short time it will be told to move. This seemed almost too civil and we found it was merely for the benefit of the Custom who wanted to seal our stores and go home, for it was getting late. A looker-on who spoke English then kindly drove me to the Harbour-master's office where the duty-man, who seemed to be slightly tiddly, advised us to berth alongside *Odinn*, the outermost of four fishery protection vessels, the whole Icelandic navy in fact. There, he assured me, we would lie undisturbed throughout our stay (*Odinn* has recently figured conspicuously in the so-called cod war.) In fact, there were two smaller vessels outside *Odinn* so we secured to the outermost. The first disturbance came before breakfast to let *Odinn* out, and the second after breakfast to let yet another similar vessel in. Meantime the topsides of *Avahur* to which we were fast were being scaled with pneumatic hammers. So we looked round for a better and quieter hole and finally went alongside a tanker, *Haforninn*, moored at a nearby wharf and apparently out of commission. We were told that ten years previously, before the herring deserted Iceland waters or had been fished to extinction, she had been employed as a sort of fleet herring-carrier and that her tanks had suffered from this misuse. She was now for sale. We found a rope-ladder by which we could gain her deck and thence access to the wharf only a few minutes' walk from the town. We lay there very comfortably with no need to tend any shore-lines, while *Haforninn* acted as a buffer between us and the occasional drunken Icelander, full of Black Death and *joie de vivre* who invites himself on board. Black Death is the appropriate name for a fiery and lethal by-product of the State brewery's non-alcoholic beer, the only beer allowed in Iceland.

This was my third call at Reykjavik and I learnt with regret that the Sailor's Home where we used to be able to get showers and cheap, abundant meals had been closed. A fine, new bath-house had been built at the far end of the docks, but for supper we had to look for cheap eating places in the town. Peter now decided to take passage home and we could not blame him. He had been ill on and off all the time, eating little, and too feeble to do any work. We had to find a replacement. The more difficult part of the voyage lay ahead, not to mention the passage homewards, and I wanted a full crew. From as far back as 1954 I had learnt that even in England suitable crew are not to be picked up like blackberries; in Iceland the chances seemed remote. The size of Reykjavik's population, some 70,000, really has no bearing because the field of choice is restricted to the small band of nomadic youngsters from Europe and America who in summer walk, hitch-hike, or bus themselves all over the island. There is a small sailing club at Reykjavik from which a recruit might be had, in which case one would either have to drop him on return, leaving one short-handed for the homeward voyage, or take him to England and pay his fare back. The yachting boom that in recent years has seen boats turned out on production lines like motor cars has not hit Iceland. There are not enough people, for the climate is not all that inimical to yachting. Nor are all yachtsmen fair-weather sun-seekers, as the offshore and ocean racing fraternity bear witness by having to take the weather as it comes. Even if in summer the Icelandic climate can be a little harsh; to offset this there are extensive and exciting cruising grounds and well-sheltered fjords.

Our search for crew did not have to be hurried. We had time in hand, for having regard to ice conditions we did not want to be off Scoresby Sound until the first week of August at the earliest. Bob and Marius made the standard tourist trip to Gulfoss and the Great Geyser, and on their return Max and Peter embarked in a bus intent on a five-day walk over the glaciated Mirdals Jokull, 70 miles south-east of Reykjavik. I remained at home. So far as tourist attractions go my feelings are those of Dr. Johnson who would have liked seeing the Giant's Causeway but would not like the trouble of going to see it.

The Youth Hostel, where there was a steady trickle of visitors, was the most likely cover to draw and there the crew made known themselves and our need. Indirectly this worked. The news got around among the foreign community and we were soon in touch with a young American, Jim Collins, who had been working on a small, local fishing boat. The boat was now laid up for repairs on account of engine trouble. According to his account Jim had been knocking about the world for three years and even after five weeks in an Icelandic fishing boat, usually a profitable occupation, his accumulated capital amounted to 10 dollars. Wishing to get to Europe he readily cast in his lot with us and we never had cause to regret it. He soon got used to our ways and proved himself a most able hand and a cheery shipmate.

Bob had an introduction to an Icelandic woman, a journalist, who very kindly asked the whole lot of us to her house for what proved to be a memorable meal, memorable at least as regards the solids. The sweet came first, an old Icelandic custom, and since it consisted of yoghourt and strawberries we had no grounds for complaint. Except, perhaps on the score of size, for having travelled through real yoghourt country in Central Asia where a normal portion is a washbasinful I found the small bowls a little meagre. After this promising opening we had salmon caught in a local river, so good that the accompanying vegetables and other trimmings hardly mattered. Unfortunately, this highly civilised meal had to be washed down with non-alcoholic beer, and there was no escaping this even on a plea of teetotalism.

In our turn we entertained a Dutchman, Dr. Hartog, who turned up one morning sailing single-handed in an aluminium-alloy 8 tonner to moor alongside us. He was not a single-hander by choice. He usually sailed with his wife, a combination that can and has resulted in famous and formidable crews, such as the Smeetons, the Hiscocks, and the late Dr. and Mrs. Pye. On this occasion he had unwisely declared his intention to reach Greenland to which his wife had responded with "Include me out" or the Dutch equivalent. The doctor had not enjoyed his lone voyage and on meeting contrary winds had put into Reykjavik prior to returning to Scotland where his wife was waiting. He may have been pining for his wife's cooking and I doubt if our curry and duff would abate this longing.

There are not many capital cities where one can walk out to the airport in twenty minutes. I walked out there frequently to talk to the Meteorological boys who were always ready to pass on what news they had of ice conditions off Greenland. This news was invariably bad, whether it came from photographs taken by satellites or from air reconnaissance. They were naturally more interested in conditions off Iceland which were unusual for that time of year, the ice lying within 30 to 40 miles off Horn, the north-western extremity of Iceland. I also had a report at first hand from a pilot whom I knew who had just flown a party to a landing strip north of Scoresby Sound. He happened, too, to be the Commodore of the Odinn Yacht Club from whom in the following year we received valuable help. He had seen heavy ice all the way to Scoresby except for a wide lead well south of it. Since at least three weeks would elapse before we were up there or thereabouts we were not unduly discouraged; nevertheless the indications were that conditions were not going to be favourable.

CHAPTER THREE

To the North

We sailed on 21st July, and since it was still full early in the season we intended calling at Isafjord, a fishing port in north-west Iceland. Iceland was enjoying a rare bout of hot weather and as one bright, cloudless day succeeded another we trusted that the ice would soon feel the effect. Glorious weather, indeed, for everything except sailing. For six days of faint northerly breezes, or no wind at all, we tacked and drifted up the coast until on the 26th a stronger breeze gave us a welcome push into the wide entrance of our fjord. There it left us. Isafjord lay 30 miles up so we started the engine. Nothing happened. The kraken, or its Icelandic equivalent, must be gripping *Seabreeze* by the keel. Bob, who was our engineer, then peered over the stern where the absence of any propeller explained her reluctance to move. We then recalled that on leaving Reykjavik under power the engine had suddenly revved up, probably signalling the shedding of the propeller; by then we were hoisting sail, having finished with the engine, and we had paid no more attention.

A few minutes before this painful discovery a local fishing boat had come alongside to present us with several fine cod, and we watched with regret as he disappeared down the fjord towards Isafjord. For a bottle of whisky they would no doubt have been delighted to give us a tow. The calm that prevailed that evening after supper looked like lasting for days. We tried towing with the dinghy but she barely moved. Then we got our two pairs of oars and a long piece of 6 in. plank—more effective than the oars—using the life-line stanchions as thole-pins. We may have had some tide with us but I reckoned that in three hours we moved her two or three miles. At 1 a.m. we gave up, for we were no Vikings. To wait for a wind, however long the wait might be, seemed preferable, a decision that Vikings themselves might have come to in the absence of women, slaves, or prisoners of war to row for them.

The calm did not last that long. By mid-morning of the next day we were in a short arm of the fjord with Isafjord close ahead. Isafjordhur, to give it its full name, is built on what is called an *eyri*, a long spit of sand and gravel. As the *Pilot* says of these parts:

> The deep-water fjords running for considerable distances south-eastwards between high steep coasts, all possess good harbours or anchorages behind an *eyri* or moraine which is peculiar to most of the Icelandic fjords. These *eyris* are low spits of shingle or sand which extend transversely across the fjord and are the remains of terminal moraines of the Ice Age.

This particular spit sticks out across the fjord to within half a cable of the other side, leaving a buoyed entrance channel with a navigable fairway of only 50 yards width. The channel is dog-legged and there are three pairs of leading marks indicating the points at which course must be altered. Another curious feature of the channel is a runway on the side opposite to the *eyri*, so that one may have a plane taxi-ing along the runway a few yards from the ship.

We had the tide under us but the wind contrary as we boldly began tacking up this narrow channel, the crew right on their toes, putting her about smartly at extremely short intervals. We were about half-way through and doing well, having hit neither the *eyri* nor the runway, when a launch came up astern and a stentorian voice asked if we needed help. It was the local pilot, also acting British consul, an ex-trawler skipper, familiar with English ports and English, and married to a Yorkshire woman. Having no false pride I gladly accepted this timely offer. With the launch made fast alongside we proceeded to the harbour while I explained to Mr. Johanssen our predicament and our immediate needs—a wall against which we could lie where at low water we would be able to get at the propeller shaft. We anchored off the jetty and after lunch, at the top of the tide, the pilot took us alongside where we warped her back until the stern took the ground. Having canted her over with the boom and put a line from the masthead to hold her, we waited for the tide to go down. In the meantime Mr. Johanssen had betrayed a liking for rum. I have never seen a man drink faster. Michael Finsbury, whom readers of *The Wrong Box* will remember, remarked admiringly of another equally fast drinker that "it restored his faith in the human race".

We found that we had not only lost our propeller but that the shaft had broken off a few inches inside the "A" bracket. One of the nuts holding this bracket had come off thus causing excessive vibration. Besides finding a suitable propeller, which looked like being difficult, a new shaft would have to be made. Without Mr. Johanssen we should not have got much done. He persuaded an engineering firm to start right away drawing the old shaft while he himself scoured the town for a left-handed propeller of the approximate size. By next day he had heard of one that belonged to the local diver who at that moment, as one might expect, was under water. Together we watched from the quayside while he cut away the trawl net that had wrapped itself round the propeller of a German trawler, the trawler having been towed in by a compatriot. That job done we went off to inspect the diver's propeller, a trifle smaller than our own and a good deal worn; we were not likely to find anything better in Isafjord and we soon came to terms over a glass of rum in *Seabreeze*'s cabin. Meantime, the engineers had had trouble drawing the broken shaft, the bolts of the gear box having seized up. To free them they used an oxyacetylene torch and succeeded, much to our surprise, before the engine caught fire. We stood by with an extinguisher just in case. Finally the shaft inside had to be cut in order to get the coupling off, and it was the Thursday evening low tide before they had withdrawn the broken shaft, not forgetting to insert a wooden plug. Nevertheless they promised the job would be done by Friday evening, a promise of some consequence because the next three days were public holidays.

At low water on Friday evening, about 7.30 p.m., they brought along the new shaft. Even the face of the foreman—whom for good reason I had christened Dismal Jimmy—showed that he was trying hard to conceal a smile of satisfaction and he very easily succeeded when they discovered that the new shaft was several inches too short. Tableau! Evidently someone, possibly Dismal himself, had blundered by forgetting that a bit of the shaft had broken off with the propeller. Their reaction to this disaster was both astonishing and admirable. Instead of throwing the job in with a promise to be back after the holidays they rushed back to the workshop to make another shaft. They had not much time, in two hours or less the water would be over the plug. Bob and I watched anxiously as the water slowly rose. When they brought back the new shaft at 10 p.m. it was an inch or two above the hole. Nothing dismayed, Dismal yanked out the plug, got the shaft in, and began tightening up with his hands under water. Then they had to go back for coupling bolts, having brought the wrong ones; but by 11 p.m. the job was done and Dismal went off to enjoy or possibly suffer the coming holidays with a well-earned shot of rum under his belt. We had plenty of rum and we needed it—a sort of Daffy's Elixir, a universal solvent and lubricant, especially in Isafjord. When Bob started the engine everything seemed to work, and at low tide next morning he put pins through the nuts of the "A" bracket to obviate their working loose again.

This north-western peninsula of Iceland known as Vestfird is pretty remote, joined to the rest of Iceland by a narrow neck only 6 miles wide; and although of considerable size the peninsula is so indented with fjords that no place on it is more than 12 miles from the sea. In this remote place visiting yachts are naturally rare and inevitably we had a great number of curious spectators gazing down at us from the jetty. Besides the natives we were inspected by a party of six American climbers bound for Scoresby Sound, needless to say by air. They did not seem to think much of our way of getting there and they may have been right. But to be carried by air to the mountains of one's choice, either in Greenland, Alaska, or even nowadays the Himalaya, as all climbing parties are, is a poor introduction. Unless told, one might not know in which continent one had arrived. Much depends on one's point of view, whether arriving or travelling hopefully is the aim. Another visitor provided me with some amusement. He was an English tourist off one of the Icelandic steamers that do the round of Iceland starting from Reykjavik. The usual questions were put—how many days from England and where were we bound for—and on being told Greenland he remarked brightly: "Ah! Following in Tilman's footsteps."

By the Saturday morning (31st July) we were ready to go. Having filled up with water, settled our debts, and paid a grateful farewell to Mr. Johanssen we cast off. Under power, with the new propeller working well, the dog-legged channel gave us no worry. Once clear we hoisted sail and beat out to sea down the main fjord. On its northern shore drifts of winter snow still lay almost down

to sea level. Before breakfast next morning we had crossed the
Arctic Circle which runs a few miles north of Horn and just fails
to touch the north coast of Iceland at any point. The island of
Grimsey, half-way along the north coast, is the only bit of Iceland
inside the Arctic Circle. The reports of ice off Horn that we had
heard at Reykjavik were confirmed next afternoon when we sighted
a line of ice to port and scattered floes ahead and to starboard.
At midnight we met the ice edge and had to go about, steering
south through scattered floes with two men on watch; for by now
the nights were getting dark. Had it been at all rough, with white
horses making the bits of ice difficult to spot we should have hove-
to. With ice about the helmsman gets out of the cockpit and stands
on deck where he can see more, but even so a look-out in the bows
is needed to warn him of ice directly ahead. In spite of steering back
towards Iceland we did not get clear of the ice until noon next
day and when visibility had improved we could still see a line of
ice to the east trending towards the coast. The air temperature
was 39°F. and the sea 36°F. so we lit the cabin stove.

This unusual accumulation of ice off the coast in August involved
us in beating about for several days before we reached open water.
An ice report that I saw subsequently showed that on 3rd August
Denmark Strait, the 300-mile wide stretch of water between
Greenland and Iceland, was completely bridged by pack-ice,
obliging a British trawler to return home south of Iceland instead
of north-about. On that particular day we were between the coast
and the south edge of the ice which still extended eastwards. The
question was how far east we should have to go to round it, for
we were already a long way off the direct course for Scoresby
Sound.

That evening, in a deserted sea, no trawlers anywhere in sight,
we again made up to the ice-edge to see what the prospects were
and found that we were about to be embayed. Standing south
with what little wind there was, we reached open water by next
morning having made good only some 14 miles to the east.
Another attempt to steer north was baffled on the morning of the
5th when once more we met the ice edge and had to sheer off to
the east yet again. But this time an easterly course took us into
more ice and for the rest of the morning we devoted ourselves
to getting into trouble with complete success. By the time fog
closed down, reducing visibility to a hundred yards, we had been

motoring for an hour or so, the floes having drawn closer together. With the wind free it is possible to sail through scattered floes, with a head wind one soon finds oneself wildly off course or with the sails aback and the boat jostling a floe. Conning the boat from up the shrouds I soon managed to get her into a cul-de-sac where, with little room for manœuvre, we spent a long time turning round. Such mistakes are costly in time. Worse still, if the ice is on the move one's retreat from the cul-de-sac may be cut off.

For two more anxious hours I conned the ship as best I could from aloft until at last I detected open water ahead. At the same time, just showing above the shallow bank of fog, I made out the crow's nest of a ship steaming slowly along the edge of the ice that we were about to break out from. We emerged from the ice just ahead of him and the slight swell we met confirmed that we were in open water. As we began hoisting sail the Norwegian whale-chaser, for such he was, closed with us for a gam. After greetings, a heaving line landed on deck and we were invited to haul away. Attached to it was the biggest lump of meat (whale meat) I have ever seen, a great block of it, 2 ft. by 2 ft. by 1 ft. thick, no bone, fat, or gristle, all prime steak.

The fog lifted, the sun came out, and as we sailed northwards we counted no less than eighteen trawlers, mostly British, fishing on the Spordagrun bank. We were thankful to be among this lot in daylight; with their trawls down they are reluctant to alter course so one does well to keep clear of trawlers, especially by night. That evening we were becalmed south of another field of ice which, when we began sailing, forced us still more to the east. In fact before we were free to steer the desired course we were in the longitude of Akureyri half-way along the north coast of Iceland. I was hoping to sight the islet of Kolbeinsey, only 26 ft. high, and was rash enough to tell the crew where to expect it, somewhere on the starboard bow. It finally showed up some 5 miles away on the port quarter, which was a pity. According to the *Pilot* Kolbeinsey lies west of its charted position; no distance is given so one is no wiser.

A good south-easterly breeze on the 7th gave us a lift northwards, the sea temperature up to 45°F., and no ice anywhere in sight. The glass was falling and next morning a strange cloud formation to the south boded mischief. So hard and firm was the outline of this sugar-loaf mountain of cloud astern that we had

3. Fending off ice from *Sea Breeze*.

4. The use of an ice bollard to secure the vessel to leeward of ice.

5. *Sea Breeze* in a west Greenland fjord.

to look long and closely before deciding that it was merely cloud. The wind freshened and we ran on close-reefed to the north-west where we soon sighted a line of ice all along the port hand. Our position, 68° 40′ N. and 19° 00′ W., put us nearly a hundred miles out from the Greenland coast, and it was disconcerting, to say the least of it, to meet ice so far from the coast. Even had we not seen the pack the drop in the sea temperature to 35°F. would have told us that it was not far away. The air temperature was 36°F. For the next two days it blew fresh from north and at night either fog or ice obliged us to heave-to. We had no reason to complain. In the Greenland sea fog, ice, and northerly winds are to be expected.

By 11th August the weather improved and by steering north true we reached 70° N., the latitude of Scoresby Sound. Accordingly we turned west. Having already seen ice a hundred miles from the coast we did not expect to make much westing and sure enough we soon descried a hard line of white stretching away to the north and to the south. On a calm, sunny evening we closed the ice to make sure, for from a few miles away scattered floes will have the appearance of an impassable wall of ice. Here were no scattered floes, but close, heavy Polar ice, an uncompromising barrier that offered no temptation to start probing, an obstacle from which one could retreat with a clear conscience. A small boat had no business there and even had the floes been fairly open we were so far from coast, a good 60 miles, that to attempt to pass through would have been foolhardy. Provided one knows what lies beyond no harm would come from attempting a passage of a few miles through scattered floes, assuming one has the sense to retreat if they start thickening. A passage of 60 miles, measured in days rather than hours, offers too many hostages to fortune in the shape of changes in the weather and the vagaries of machinery. Sailing among floes is not easy and to find oneself a few miles inside the pack with a broken-down engine might have all kinds of consequences, none of them pleasant. The Greenland whaling fleet worked among ice as a matter of course, ships of 300 to 400 tons massively built with crews of forty to fifty men of a kind that is not bred nowadays. Most important of all, they cruised in company so that if one were beset help or a refuge was at hand.

To satisfy ourselves that there were no open leads or that the ice did not suddenly fall away to the west, we went north for

c

another 20 miles only to see it stretching away into the distance as far as the eye could see. There remained only to follow the ice edge south on the chance of finding an inshore lead in a lower latitude, an unwelcome decision that meant throwing away our hard-won northing. As we went south the hard edge gave away to loose floes, sometimes in the form of capes projecting from the main pack. Fog on the 13th made for despondency but when it lifted the next day a clear horizon all round gave our spirits a wonderful lift. The only ice in sight was a solitary berg. After a moderate gale had obliged us to heave-to a fine easterly breeze encouraged us to steer west to close the ice. We were about in Lat. 68° 5′ N. or 70 miles south-east of C. Brewster at the southern entrance to the Sound. With no ice in sight ahead we began steering direct for the cape but by noon we were again among scattered floes with the hard edge of the pack showing all too clearly to the north. We spent the night hove-to and next day began motoring due west through fairly open ice. We went on into the ice for some 6 miles before prudence prevailed. Conditions were no easier and there was every possibility that we would be motoring through ice all the way to the coast. Nor was there any certainty of finding ice-free water along the coast had we reached it, a process that would have involved something like twenty-four hours of motoring. My faith in machinery hardly extends that far and we had on board no mechanical genius capable of dealing with any emergency. An Indian driver I once had shared my incompetence with machinery and the consequent lack of faith in it. When the truck broke down, as it frequently did, all he could find to say was: "It is but machinery, Sahib."

Steering south did not get us out of the ice as we had expected. We had to retrace our steps to the east and did not win clear until late that night—a mis-spent day if ever there was one. So far as Scoresby Sound went we had shot our bolt. It was evidently a bad ice year and we had to accept defeat. "Prudence", as Dr. Johnson says, "quenches that ardour of enterprise by which everything is done that can claim praise or admiration," but Dr. Johnson was no mariner upon whom caution and prudence are enjoined. Instead we decided to sail direct to Angmagssalik to stock up for the homeward passage, before going on to one of the many mountainous fjords further south for the brief time that remained.

CHAPTER FOUR

Angmagssalik and Homewards

For the next two days we were constantly edged away to the east of our desired course by ice of various kinds, big floes, growlers, and bergy bits, evidently the lingering remains of what had recently been close-pack-ice. Such bits of ice generally show up white and are easy to see, but not all of them. On a calm, clear night, as we were sailing along quietly, a piece of ice about 15 ft. long, completely awash, nothing showing, only betrayed its presence a few feet from the hull by the waves slapping against it. This happening in my watch gave me a salutary shock and towards the end of the next day I was to have another. During the first watch that morning, blowing fresh and snowing, the boat had a real Arctic appearance with snow lying about the deck and encasing the shrouds. We did 12 miles in that watch. As the day advanced the wind increased and the snow turned to rain with visibility not more than half a mile. Anxious to make up for lost time we let her rip, sailing full and by with all plain sail, running her off to south-east during the frequent heavy squalls. For the last few days, since we were far from land, particularly from Greenland, I had been navigating on a plotting chart, a blank sheet except for the lines of latitude and longitude. So at 4 p.m. when I was below, enjoying tea and wads, the cry of "Land" from on deck gave me a rude shock. Sure enough close to windward through the murk loomed a gaunt cliff with a solitary house at its foot.

A glance at the appropriate chart would have shown that on the course we were steering and the rate we were going we should soon be nearing Horn, and that the frequency with which we had been obliged to run her off still more to the east would ensure our fetching up on the wrong side of it, as indeed we had. At this awkward moment the wind increased in violence. Nevertheless we had to gybe, which we did without breaking anything, and were relieved to see that grim headland fade away in the rain. Overnight the barometer rose 10 mbs. and the wind moderated. By morning the wind had swung round to the east and by noon we had rounded Horn and soon left Iceland astern.

Denmark Strait, which on earlier voyages had been placid enough, seemed in a disturbed state. Again the wind increased until by midnight we had reefed down so far that only some six feet of luff remained on the mast. Rain set in, and when an iceberg showed up with its litter of bergy bits stretching for hundreds of yards to leeward, we hove-to. As a general rule one should pass up-wind of icebergs. In a hard blow, even when close-reefed, *Seabreeze* will not lie still, but makes almost a knot crabwise, so what with the way she had on and the breaking seas that made ice difficult to see we passed an anxious day and a worse night. For by night, though the wind had dropped, we were enveloped in fog, and more than once that night a fearful thump and the trample of feet overhead would announce that the watch on deck were fending off a chunk of ice. In the persisting fog I became concerned to know where we were until at last on 23rd August, through rifts in the fog, I got both a morning and a noon sight. They were not easy to take. After waiting patiently on deck for the horizon under the sun to clear, no sooner had one brought up the sextant than in the cold atmosphere the mirrors misted over. By now, of course, the nights were quite dark, and what with fog and the presence of icebergs we kept double watches.

We were nearing Greenland, and at length the sort of weather that I have come to associate with the east coast set in—flawless, windless, sunny days when the calm blue water reflects the majestic shapes of glistening icebergs. On 25th August we sighted the coast, marvellously mountainous and wonderfully clear even at 40 miles distance. We were north of Angmagssalik and of C. Dan where the coast recedes abruptly to the west. This marked turning away of the coast makes the cape easy to identify and besides that it has on it the only radio beacon on the coast. Having no RDF equipment we were more concerned to see it than to hear it, and the big, silvery domes are easily seen from a distance.

By evening we were south of the cape and heading west in search of Angmagssalik. This is less readily found. One steers for a bold, brown promontory that looks like the end of the land, where the coast makes another sharp turn to the west. The promontory is steep-to and can be approached safely, and one needs to be close to make out the narrow entrance to King Oscar's Havn or the small, dimly lit beacon on its northern side. The harbour lies about a mile inside the entrance and is small, small enough to be congested even by the few diminutive local vessels that are usually there. So we anchored outside near the root of the breakwater within a few yards of the rocky shore and some brightly painted Greenlander huts. It was near midnight when we let go the anchor to a chorus of howls from all the huskies in the town—a bright, clear night with the aurora shimmering overhead like a curtain of pale fire.

We were last here in *Mischief* in 1965 since when the town has grown—a new wharf and warehouse at the harbour, more roads, more houses, and more shops. Then there had been only the one store, that run by the Royal Greenland Trading Co. which used to have the monopoly of all trade in Greenland; now there are several privately-owned shops and even a coffee-bar complete with juke-box and fruit machine. The Greenlanders—the men at any rate—are happy-go-lucky, free spenders, and born gamblers; the fruit machine seemed to suffer accordingly, taking a hard and incessant pounding. The helpful Danish Harbour-master who had been here in 1965 was no more, his place having been taken by a Greenlander, while the shipwright carpenter who had patched up *Mischief* after her passage through the ice, was away on leave. The local boat *Ejnar Mikelsen*, which on that occasion had helped us through the ice, had been replaced by a new version under the same skipper, our good friend Niels Underborg. He and I had a long gam. He told me that another English boat, a converted motor fishing vessel with a crew of twelve, mostly mountaineers, had called and that he had taken them up the coast to Kangerdlugssual. As far as that apparently the coast had been almost ice-free, while north of that, as we had found, the ice spread far to the east.

Max went off on a solitary glacier walk while the rest of us busied ourselves with repairs to the mainsail, turning halyards end for end, and putting a tingle over a suspected leak under the counter. For old time's sake I went up what we used to call Spy-glass hill. This was the hill just behind the town, close on 2,000 ft. high, that on our first slightly hazardous visit in 1964 we climbed frequently, sometimes before breakfast, in order to see if the ice in the offing had opened sufficiently for us to escape. Having got into Angmagssalik early that year, with the essential help of *Ejnar Mikelsen* and the springing of some planks as well, we were then unable to leave and had been held prisoners by the ice for three weeks. From Spy-glass hill one had been able to see what the ice conditions out to sea were like, but this time, instead of time spent on reconnaissance being never wasted, it almost invariably was wasted. For having rushed down the hill back to the boat, got under way, motored down the fjord, and arrived on the scene, one found that the ice had moved and that the wide lead spotted from Spy-glass hill no longer existed.

Having gone alongside in the harbour for water we sailed on 29th August bound for Sehesteds fjord about a hundred miles to the south. The *Pilot* thus describes the fjord:

> Sehesteds fjord extends about 23 miles north-westwards with several branches. At its head are mountains which reach an elevation of as much as 6,700 ft. On the northern side is a narrow inlet named Rans Sund which is reported to afford good anchorage for small craft. In August 1932 the *Veslekari* anchored in Rans Sund and observed that new ice began to form in the harbour on 11th August.

Rans Sund then seemed to be the place to make for, and one could only hope that the formation of new ice in August was the exception rather than the rule. Seldom can so short a passage have taken so long—five aggravating days, the wind light and fitful, pestered by bergs, and rolling horribly for a lot of the time in a quite unaccountable swell. Big sailing ships lying becalmed were said to draw together by some sort of mutual attraction. The same thing happened as we lay becalmed near a big iceberg, only we drew together so fast that we imagined the berg to be self-propelled and bent on running us down. There were at least fifty bergs in sight that morning and the largest of them, a real monster, lay close at hand. Seeing that he was drawing uncomfortably near we started the engine and headed out to sea to get clear. It is hard to believe—and we had not lost our propeller this time—

but for a good ten minutes neither the bearing nor our distance from this brute appreciably altered. We felt we were being pursued. However, he was not as quick on the helm as we were and by altering course to south-west we shook him off.

By 2nd September we were, I hoped, about off the entrance to our fjord, some 7 miles out from the land. Like the rest of Greenland the coast here abounds in fjords, off-lying islands, islets, and skerries, all unmarked. Identification is difficult and in our case was essential. Owing to the absence of any features that could be described as "unmistakable" or even "remarkable" the *Pilot*'s description of the coast hereabouts did not much help. Of the numerous capes mentioned the added characteristic of "bold", or "brown", or "steep reddish-brown" seemed to fit most of them. Meantime we were being thrown about by a very lively swell that ran in all directions and for which there was no accounting. It would be a relief to gain the quiet waters of the fjord but before closing the land I wanted to be sure of our latitude. It was near noon and though the sky was overcast we waited in hope. The sun duly obliged and now that we knew our latitude for certain the distant scene began to fall into shape like the pieces of a jigsaw puzzle.

So we started the engine and the next few hours of motoring through that infernal lop were my idea of hell. The violent swell, big enough at times to lift our propeller clear of the water, reduced our speed to a crawl, and as it broke against the numerous bergs sheets of spray were flung into the air. A great deal of camera film was wasted on this impressive spectacle, for the breaking waves offered a target as fleeting as that of a surfacing dolphin. Some skerries at the fjord entrance were not shown on the chart and Bob, who pointed this out, was convinced we were in the wrong fjord. I myself had some doubts. Except for the immense number of floes that cluttered the surface it looked remarkably like Skjoldungen, the next fjord to the north which we had visited in 1965. These doubts were soon dispelled, the features agreed with the chart, and some ten miles up we boldly took a short cut into Rans Sund by way of a narrow gut. Like most short cuts it would have been better avoided, encumbered as it was with rocks and ice floes. Great was my relief when we emerged safely into Rans Sund, a lovely anchorage, spacious but sheltered, free from ice, a stream for watering, and two fine peaks within striking distance.

A solitary seal and a couple of wheatears were the only signs of life.

The higher of the two peaks, which was also the furthest away, at once attracted Max. To climb it from the boat would be a longish day and since its lower slopes were hidden by intervening ground he decided to make sure of it by taking a camp. I tried to dissuade him and urged him to devote the first day to the nearest peak whence he would almost certainly see enough of the other to decide on the best route. I suspect Max wanted an excuse for carrying a load and camping on snow. Anyhow, the advice of the super-annuated mountaineer was not taken with the result that both peaks remained unclimbed.

The climbing party, Max and Jim, left at 9 a.m. next day, 3rd September. The rest of us had sails to mend, the main sheet to turn, water to get, and finally to build a large cairn on the beach. The rain that set in at midday continued all night and most of the following morning by which time everything above 500 ft. was plastered with snow. This augured ill for the success of the climbers. The glass fell to 985 mbs. Even with a companion, or if the snow had not fallen, or Jim had not borrowed my ice-axe, I think the nearer peak would have been beyond my reach. I got only as far as a col on the long ridge leading to the summit. Below the col some six inches of new snow lay on top of hard ice so that without an axe I had to take to the neighbouring rocks. Thick mist obscured everything except when through an occasional rift I had a glimpse of the fjord and *Seabreeze* far below. Having waited in vain for two hours I started down when, of course, the mist began to disperse, revealing on the far side of the fjord two noble glaciers. The climbers got back at 7 p.m. On the previous day they had camped on a glacier at the foot of their mountain and on the following morning a complete white-out had prevented their doing anything but strike camp and stumble back down the glacier as best they could. Max had no regrets. He has the right idea about mountains—happy to be among them, preferably camping, even if he can't be on top of them.

The cat-ice that formed overnight on the still water of our anchorage hinted that summer was over and that it was time for us to go. Early in the morning as we sailed down the fjord the rising sun tinged the high peaks astern of us with a warm Alpine glow. Offshore the swell still ran though with reduced violence and as we sped eastwards with a fair wind the almost unknown mountains of this splendid coast faded in the distance. That night, in spite of a brilliant full moon, we watched a vivid display of aurora when for nearly five hours the northern sky was lit by long shafts and flickering curtains of pale green fire. Next day we sighted our last berg, fully a hundred miles out from the coast.

The gremlin that lurked in the spars of *Seabreeze* was still there. The spars had always been in trouble. On her first voyage with me in 1969 the topmast, bowsprit, and gaff all broke, the first two early in the voyage, the last on the way home. In 1970 the mended gaff broke again and now the same spar, once more scarfed, broke for the third time. In spite of this I had great confidence in the mast, the most important of all, which was a good inch thicker than *Mischief*'s mast, as well as in the boom which was nearly as thick as the mast. The gaff broke on the afternoon of the 12th when a German tanker altered course to have a look at us and passed a cable's length away. With a farewell blast of the horn she sheered off and a minute or so later our bow hit a wave with some violence, a wave that was probably caused by the tanker's wash. The gaff promptly broke, snapping clean in two. Having handed and lashed the mainsail we set the tops'l abaft the mast like a trys'l.

Colin Putt, the make-do and mend maestro of the previous voyage, would have enjoyed himself, but between them the crew seemed well able to cope, Bob providing the brains and Max the brawn. He spent most of one day hammering stubborn pieces of metal tubing flat and bending them to the required shape. These were brackets designed to hold in place the two wooden splints, 6 ft. lengths of 3 in. by 3 in. By the following day all was ready for assembly, a tricky job since the spar was in two separate pieces, not merely sprung; while the rolling of the boat, with no steadying mainsail, made it difficult to line up the two pieces. The gaff had evidently outlived its usefulness—a new one would certainly be needed—so we had no mercy on the old one, driving into it through the splints a great number of 6 in. nails. The final nail driven, we unlashed the mainsail and hoisted; what a joy it was to feel the boat respond, her customary liveliness restored. Although I bet Bob a pint or two that his gaff would not last, I had little doubt that it would see us home.

In spite of this delay and yet another when the mainsail had to come down again to splice the broken leach rope, we made a fast passage. By the 16th we were within 600 miles of Mizzen Head, beginning to meet Irish gannets, and practically in home waters. Once more we resumed the bad habit of listening to shipping forecasts and by changing ship's time to British Summer Time found ourselves having breakfast by candle-light. On the 23rd we passed a fine Russian passenger ship without any passengers, and early on the following night we picked up the Bishop light. Even in the Channel we met neither fog nor head winds. By 27th September we were in Lymington river receiving from the Royal Lymington clubhouse the finishing gun, their customary generous salute on our return.

CHAPTER FIVE

1972. A Change of Plan

That the account of this voyage is not as full as it should be is partly owing to the absence of records and partly to that convenient faculty the mind has of forgetting what it does not wish to remember. That this faculty of forgetting is not at all times absolute many of us no doubt regret when some of the unfortunate or unworthy incidents from our past involuntarily come to mind.

Although in 1971 we had had an enjoyable and comparatively trouble-free voyage we had failed to reach our objective and had not achieved anything elsewhere. For us Scoresby Sound remained inviolate, unseen even from afar, and no Greenland mountain had been climbed. I began to feel that in trying to reach Scoresby Sound we were "standing for some false, impossible shore, still bent to make some port he knows not where". The odds against a small boat reaching the Sound are long and, as we found in 1971, the attempt has to be made so late in the summer that failure leaves too little time for the carrying out of any alternative plan.

My thoughts reverted to west Greenland, particularly the northern part which is, of course, much further away. There, one was more likely to be defeated by distance than by ice. In 1963 we had followed the west coast up as far as Upernivik (72° 47′ N.) with little trouble and had then crossed Baffin Bay to Bylot Island in Lat. 73° N. The ice we met had been easily avoided nor was there much of it, for that part of Baffin Bay is what the whaling men called the North Water, a large piece of ice-free water or polynia. The reasons why this particular area should be free of ice are not fully understood. Beyond Baffin Bay in Lat. 76° N. is the south coast of Ellesmere Island, highly glaciated, mildly mountainous, and sufficiently remote to be of great interest if one got there. A number of geologists, glaciologists, and the like

43

do go there, and Mr. Hattersley Smith, a friend of mine who knew the island well, strongly recommended it to me; he also provided the necessary Canadian charts and maps.

Obviously this was an ambitious project, for it is a long way north, though on the whole the chances of carrying it out compared favourably, I think, with those of reaching Scoresby Sound. Anyway, why start for a place that is almost certain to be reached? The first requisite, an able boat, was at hand, for after three voyages *Seabreeze* was getting into good shape. The new gaff had been made a half-inch thicker than the old one and she also had a new mainsail of heavy flax canvas, roped all round. One's whims must be paid for. Compared with terylene, from which sails are made nowadays, flax canvas is heavy and therefore harder to hoist, is less immune to mildew and rot and therefore cannot be stowed away wet. It is also less durable, less durable, that is, in temperate climates—terylene will not stand too much hot sun. On the other hand flax canvas is in keeping with a boat built in 1899, is cheaper, and when flapping in the wind does not crackle like a machine gun. Quietness is worth buying.

The deck had been treated with a heavy, viscous paint which went some way to stopping the drips. No doubt, re-caulking, an expensive operation, would have stopped them entirely. Besides this, improvements had been made below, particularly in the galley which Brian Potter had now reorganised to his liking: Brian had been cook on the first eventful and disappointing voyage in *Seabreeze*, and he was sailing again in what proved to be her last. He is an efficient sea-cook but, as a craftsman in wood-work, is more interested in making things, so that jobs like fitting shelves, cupboards, plate racks, while hardly taxing his skill are done with gusto, *con amore*. During the winter we had put in several week-ends together, sometimes with Colin Putt, another ex-crew, who had undertaken the overhaul of the engine and the making of a new exhaust pipe. In the theory and practice of machinery of any size or degree, from a tractor to a clockwork train, I regard Colin as the maestro. Had he been sailing with us it is highly probable that the voyage would not have ended as it did.

The second recruit for this voyage was a Richard Capstick who was contemplating throwing up his job as Industrial correspondent of the *Daily Mail* in Hull. Besides its own telephone system, I believe Hull has its own *Daily Mail*. He was not without experience

having done some ocean racing, and that he had some enterprise
he showed by making a trip in a Hull trawler to Iceland in the early
spring before joining *Seabreeze*. I took the precaution of meeting
him in London beforehand, but such interviews are not much to
the purpose for gauging a man's fitness for life in a small boat
along with four other strangers. For me they merely ensure that
when the man turns up at Lymington and says he has come to
join one can believe him; not invariably because my memory
for faces is not that good and in this case, since our first meeting,
the man had grown a beard. Expedition experience, which is seldom
forthcoming, would be a fairly sure means of finding out whether
a man will turn out well or ill, for one can enquire from those who
were with him how he shaped.

The third candidate I had not even the slight advantage of
seeing before he joined. Like Max Smart of the previous voyage
I took him simply on the recommendation of a friend whose
judgement could be relied upon, an act of considerable faith since
Brian McClanagan, the man in question, had no experience either
of sailing or climbing. He was then in Australia and would not be
able to join until a few days before sailing. In recent years I
have probably had more offers of crew from Australia and New
Zealand than from England.

My last recruit, picked up at the last moment in a great hurry,
when someone else had dropped out, was another New Zealander.
Mike Clare had been recommended to me earlier on so that when
this unexpected vacancy occurred I had him to fall back on. He
was working at Llanberis and consequently easily met, and only
two days before I was due at Lymington to start fitting out we
foregathered at Portmadoc. Mike was eager to come, had no ties,
and the people he was working for, making mountaineering iron-
mongery, were entirely sympathetic. Besides climbing he had
had some experience of boats in New Zealand.

Enough work remained in spite of what had been done at week-
ends during the winter, while the unsettled weather in May did
not help. The new mainsail when set looked a picture, the new
gaff it hung from looked worthy of it, and the boom, we thought,
quite indestructible. Since our objective, Ellesmere Island, was
a long way off we proposed starting earlier than usual. 27th May,
the Saturday of Whit week-end, had been fixed for sailing day.
Even without the help of the shipping forecast anyone could have

guessed that the weather for going down Channel with a green, untried crew would be far from favourable. However, ships and crews rot in port so I decided to sail as planned and to anchor in the Solent to await better times. We had a long wait. For three whole days we lay there while with monotonous regularity the shipping forecast issued gale warnings for every sea area around the British Isles. It blew pretty fresh even in the Solent where we lay at anchor near the Lymington Spit buoy watching the Lyming-ton–Yarmouth ferry-boat cross and re-cross. There was little else to watch. We were rolling heavily and in Lymington it was reported that we were lying there so that the crew could get their sea-legs. Bad though the weather might be, on this holiday week-end quite a few yachts were prepared to brave it, scurrying about with only a reefed mainsail set.

On the 31st we got our anchor and sailed, the wind moderate but still at west. While beating up to the Needles we gave ourselves a severe fright by staying too long on the port tack thus getting close to the Shingles bank on the north side. Gripped by an eddy *Seabreeze* spun completely round to face the way she had come, the sails all aback. The lop left by the recent rough weather coupled with a fresh head wind made for slow progress and we tacked over to Swanage Bay to wait there until the ebb tide early next morning. When another westerly gale brewed up as we were nearing the Start I thought we might cheat it by anchoring in the lee of Start Point. To get there we sailed round the north end of the Skerries Bank which is marked by a buoy. Having rounded this we needed the engine to make up to the anchorage close inshore in the teeth of the rising wind. So frightful was the clattering noise which ensued that we quickly stopped the engine, hoisted the sails, and went back round the buoy to spend the night hove-to in Lyme Bay. In the course of the night we lost some ten miles of hard-earned westing. By then we had found that the alarming clatter originated from the companion-way steps which were backed with sheet metal.

After passing between Land's End and the Scillies we did better and by 5th June were south of Mizzen Head. Then progress became fitful. A series of depressions, none of them severe, kept us always hard on the wind and seldom pointing in the required direction. We made more northing than westing. When the choice between two evils is nicely balanced, when whichever tack is chosen means pointing 50° off the proper course, the port tack is probably the best. By so doing one is steering approximately a Great Circle course and the further north one goes the shorter the degrees of longitude.

Thus when we had already reached the latitude of C. Farewell (59° 46' N.) on 19th June we were still some 500 miles east of it. While on watch that evening Mike noticed a very slight crack in our indestructible boom. The gremlin had struck again. The slight crack did not seem to threaten immediate disaster so instead of getting the sail off, as we should have done, Brian went to work fashioning some metal bands to be bolted on. The weather then took a hand by obliging us to reef down and to remain reefed for the next thirty-six hours. However many tight rolls of canvas there may be round a cracked boom they are not much good as splints, as one might suppose. The boom assumed an ominous bend and when we began unreefing and took out the last roll it broke clean through. The mainsail, when unbent and with difficulty manhandled below, occupied most of the fore part of the boat. Having lashed the remains of the boom on deck we set the tops'l abaft the mast as we had on the previous voyage. With the weather we were having I rather funked setting the mainsail loose-footed as it could not be reefed. It meant the whole sail or nothing. None of us had suspected a weakness in the boom or dreamt that it would break, nor did anyone, I think, who had seen that massive spar. Size is not everything; the bigger they are the harder they fall. Breaking booms, I have heard, was alleged to be a fault of Pilot cutters in their working day; it was attributed to the roller-reefing gear which necessitates the main sheet (where all the strain comes) being attached to the boom at only one point and that at the extreme end of a spar that might be 30 ft. in length.

Under jury rig it would take a long time to round C. Farewell and besides that we were not likely to have a new boom made or the old one repaired anywhere in Greenland. Reykjavik, still some 300 miles to the north, seemed the best bet, although our going there would probably mean changing our plans. As the great Von Moltke used to remind his staff, few plans withstand contact with the enemy. By this time, too, I suspected that Richard intended leaving at the first opportunity and if it came at a Greenland port there would be no hope of finding a replacement.

The winds now were mostly northerly and north-westerly,

reasonably favourable for C. Farewell, but no good for Reykjavik
in our lame condition. After beating for three days, sailing about
180 miles, we had made good to the north only some 30 miles.
I became concerned about our water supply. Brian used it with
strict economy, certainly less than 3 gallons a day, but one or two
of the crew had a habit of drawing it off in the night watches.
Water needs to be husbanded on a longish voyage, the supply
being limited and unforeseen delays always possible. No water is
drunk except as tea or coffee, and those who shave may do so
only if they don't do it too often. Washing, either of plates, pots,
or persons, is done in sea water. At this time we suffered another
minor misfortune for which I blamed myself. The rigging screw
on the forestay, a vital piece of the standing rigging, came adrift,
its barrel falling into the sea. The barrel had been wired to prevent
its unscrewing but no one had kept an eye on the wire. At sea
there are very few things that one can fit and forget. With a
block on the stemhead to lead a rope to the anchor winch we set
up the stay reasonably taut.

Then we had a stroke of luck. One fine, calm afternoon we
noticed a vessel ahead, bound nowhere apparently with any urgency.
She proved to be a French fishery research vessel, *Thessala* of
Brest, bound ultimately for Rockall. The skipper, noticing our
queer rig, closed us to enquire if we needed anything. When we
mentioned water he manœuvred skilfully alongside, large fenders
out, and one man with a fender detailed specially to watch our
bowsprit. Warps were passed to make fast, then a small hosepipe,
and finally a yard or so of French bread. Having filled five jerrycans, a good ten days' supply, we cast off and went our respective
ways. There were a number of bearded marine biologists on
board, or at least we concluded they were something other than
sailors.

Emboldened by this lucky encounter we began setting the mainsail without a boom. Since it could not be reefed we had to
watch the weather, especially at night, and besides that the heavy
triple block on the clew and the direct pull of the mainsheet did
the sail no good. Meantime, Richard's inconcealed impatience to
reach Reykjavik confirmed our suspicions. Sea-cook Brian had
suspected him almost from the start on the rather flimsy grounds
that he refused to eat sardine spines and wore a yachting cap.
I felt that a man with the unseamanlike habit of wearing gloves

at night in summer in the Atlantic would not prosper on a voyage of this kind.

Even with the mainsail, which we were able to set nearly all the time, we were not off Reykjavik until 2nd July, thirty-six days out from Lymington. Since the breaking of the boom twelve days before we had made good 300 miles, having sailed many more than that in the process. Not expecting to be anywhere near Iceland on this trip I had bought no Iceland charts, nor for that matter any charts of east Greenland which it now seemed we might need. In spite of our previous visit I made a mess of the approach to Reykjavik by standing towards it from the west instead of from the north. We presently found ourselves in shoaling water, surrounded by the buoys of a regular web of fishing nets, and too close to a reef that was barely awash. Here was a situation where good advice would have been worth much but instead of that the engine stopped. It stopped for the very good reason that the fuel tank had run dry. To right this involved the lengthy and complicated process of "bleeding", and young Brian, our inexperienced engineer, confessed himself at a loss. Meantime we had got some sails set in a hurry and headed out to sea. The wind had freshened and in order to make sure of fetching the harbour on the next tack we went about four miles. While we were beating back towards the harbour Mike had a go at the "bleeding" process and succeeded beyond our hopes. Helped by the engine we weathered the point and by evening were safely secured to the quay. The tanker against which we had lain the previous year had gone. We occupied her vacant berth alongside the quay with the inconvenience of having to tend our warps.

CHAPTER SIX

North from Iceland

In Reykjavik the Customs people are fussy but friendly. After sealing up our liquor they stayed yarning until nearly midnight and on leaving they promised to telephone my air pilot friend, the Commodore of the Odinn Yacht Club. I wanted some advice as to where the boom could be repaired. He himself could not come, but next morning a club member arrived bringing with him the owner of a small boat-building yard. Taking the boom away to his yard to examine properly he returned that evening to report that in his opinion the boom could not be repaired. He proposed making a new one by laminating together eight 1 in. planks, the job to be finished by the end of the week. To this I agreed.

With that fixed we had only the delicate question of Richard's future and that settled itself almost as speedily. That afternoon Brian and I were on deck chewing the cud, discussing this and that, and among other things Richard's shortcomings, perhaps in terms less than civil. Richard, who must have already made up his mind, was below packing his voluminous gear. He evidently overheard us. Coming on deck to announce his immediate departure he touched briefly and rudely on some of our shortcomings, particularly Brian's, but for whom, he said, he would have gladly remained. Four months is not an eternity. I always warn prospective crew that however much they may come to hate me or each other, such sentiments will have to be suppressed until the end of the voyage, and that the success of the venture and the welfare of the ship come before any personal feelings. Richard, however, would not have stuck it out anyway.

Once more we were obliged to make known our want in all likely quarters, particularly at the Youth Hostel where in summer there is a steady stream of tourists of the younger and more active kind. It would be expecting too much to pick such another winner as we had the previous year in the shape of Jim Collins, the American. We did, however, hook another American. Late one evening as I sat on deck musing on the vicissitudes of life I was haled by a long, lanky figure gazing down from the quay through outsize spectacles. Invited on board the boat (then lying a long way below the level of the quay), he groped tentatively with his feet for the ratlines, missed them, hung by his hands for a brief space, before landing on deck with a portentous thud. It occurred to me then that if he were a prospective crew, of the 70,000 odd inhabitants of Reykjavik at that time, the one least likely to make a sailor had come on board. John Lapin said he was a student from California, a student of agriculture. To make sure I had the name right and to air my French I suggested John Rabbit, to which he assented, his French being as good or perhaps better than mine. He was on his way to Ireland to visit friends. He had no sea experience but was game to try and since so far all coverts had been drawn blank I took him on. "Mortal men", as Falstaff said in reply to disparaging remarks about his recruits, "Mortal men, they'll fill a pit as well as better." No sooner had I committed myself to John Lapin than Brian received a cable from a friend suggesting that his son should fly out to join us. According to Brian father was a keen and experienced yachtsman. About the son, whom he had never met, he was a little vague, thought he must be in the early twenties and no doubt as keen as father if less experienced. With this yachting paragon on offer I could only kick myself for having taken on an agriculturalist.

The boatyard were as good as their word. On the Saturday, six days after our arrival, they brought the new boom, shipped it, and gave it a preliminary coat of varnish. They had done a good job at about half of what it would have cost in an English yard. By this time I had become reconciled to giving up the west coast of Greenland, Baffin Bay, and Ellesmere Island. I reckoned we should not get there before the middle of August, a highly optimistic estimate, leaving a brief two weeks before having to start back. Instead, since we were still east of C. Farewell, we might as well stay there and make another attempt, the third, at reaching Scoresby Sound. I had already provided the necessary charts. Meantime, as it was still early in the season and we did not want to be there until early in August, we could visit Jan Mayen. This island is in approximately the same latitude as Scoresby Sound (70° N.) and only some 300 miles to the east. We had lost *Mischief* there in 1968, but forewarned is forearmed.

Accordingly we sailed on 10th July. Sailed, perhaps, is not quite the right word. With a fresh breeze blowing straight on to the quay *Seabreeze* showed great reluctance to leave it. After a lot of futile manœuvring and bumping against the quay we slowly moved out crabwise under the eyes of a large and critical audience. Worse was to follow, worse at least for our new hand John Lapin who remained on deck only briefly before retiring groaning to his bunk. There for the next five days he lay as if in a coma, a bandage over his eyes, neither eating nor drinking, not even moving. After the lapse of three or four days, when he still showed no sign of life, it became clear that we should have to land him. Whether or not his seasickness was chronic, like that of Peter Marsh, he obviously had no intention of trying to overcome it. Nothing would rouse him.

> Now my weary eyes I close
> Leave, ah, leave me, to repose.

Fortunately our progress up the coast had been slow. We had not yet passed Isafjord where he could be conveniently put ashore and where Brian could telephone to his friend about the son. The changing and inconsistent moods of sea have not escaped remark. On the previous voyage nothing could have been more tranquil and untroubled than the sea at the entrance to the fjord, while at this time it seemed to boil, white water breaking all round and well inside the fjord. Even when the light wind had died to nothing the sea continued to break. There must have been a strong tide running. With the engine going flat out it took us all our time to make over to the southern shore where we anchored for the night. Iceland fjords are less sheer-sided than those of Greenland. To my surprise we got bottom in 10 fathoms a good fifty yards out from the shore. Even the noise of the cable running out and the unwonted stillness that followed failed to rouse our passenger about whose presence on board we had almost forgotten. He might have been dead. Nevertheless, he was alive enough to realise that his short voyage was not quite over and that until then, like Brer Rabbit his namesake, his cue was to lie low and say nothing. And no sooner had we secured alongside at Isafjord next morning than he was up on deck, his gear packed, and looking remarkably well considering his five days' ordeal.

One of our earliest visitors was our pilot friend, Mr. Johanssen. I got out the rum. But he had with him his wife, who refused to come on board and refused to be left on the quay. As Sancho said, "A wife's counsel is bad but he who will not take it is mad." After a severe mental struggle Mr. Johanssen gave in, resolving not to leave her alone on the quay. Brian lost no time in going ashore to telephone to England and find out if his friend's son was still available. He was our last hope, we would find no volunteers in Isafjord, so that I was greatly relieved when Brian reported that the young man would be with us in three days' time. Brian, I noticed, took the news thoughtfully, his responsibility for introducing this unknown quantity lying heavy upon him.

The sights of Isafjord are soon exhausted. On the third day after our arrival Brian and I went for a walk up the hill which towers high over the town. We hit on a road that led to a ski-lift, the ascent gradual, the surface smooth. Even so I nearly succumbed to an attack of mountaineer's foot, and it was not until we struck up on to the ridge over rough and steep going that I felt better. On top of the ridge we had the satisfaction of setting foot on the more or less eternal snow, the height being not far short of two thousand feet. In the distance across the fjord we could see the Drangajökull, a sort of miniature ice-cap over 3,000 ft. high. Descending the other side of the ridge we found our way back to the town and so to the boat where we learnt that our new hand, Dougal Forsyth, had already arrived and had gone shopping. And rather to Brian's dismay we also learnt that he was a schoolboy of sixteen and that his experience extended only as far as Poole Bay. This piece of news shook me, too. While I myself might be too old I certainly thought sixteen to be too young for this kind of voyage and would not willingly set out from England with anyone of that age on board. However, he undoubtedly had father's consent, if not more, and it was too late to demur. When he did show up young Dougal looked uncommonly sturdy for his age and had no qualms on his own part about his suitability. For the short time the voyage lasted he did very well and looked like making a useful hand.

On 18th July, the day after Dougal's arrival, we sailed for Jan Mayen. Besides filling up time, or rather allowing time, as we hoped, for the ice off Scoresby Sound to clear, I expected to meet there a Danish friend, a member of a Danish expedition to the island. In a letter to me before his departure for Jan Mayen, where he was to be in charge of the commissariat, he had asked about the making of chapatties on a Primus stove. Chapatties are merely a dough of flour and water beaten between the palms of the hands until wafer thin and slapped on to a hot plate for a minute or two. Thinness is all important otherwise the outside is burnt black before the inside is cooked. Eaten hot, with butter oozing out, they are food for the gods as any traveller in the Himalaya would agree. On an expedition the beginner might find a bottle available as a rolling pin and even something that might serve as a board if the party is not travelling austerely; but the professional would scorn such aids and so should the aspiring amateur. All the skill and half the fun lies in achieving a paper-thin round of dough—not shaped like a map of Scotland—about the size of a plate, before it falls to pieces or wraps itself round one's wrist. Cooking it on a Primus is not easy as the heat is too fierce; over hot ashes is best. So much for chapatties.

We had no trouble with ice off Horn this year. We sighted the edge of the pack to the north-west, further away from the coast than in 1971, and had an uneventful passage. On 25th July, from a good 40 miles away, we made out the bold, black cliff at the southern extremity of Jan Mayen, the bowsprit happily pointing straight at it. With no lowering, leaden sunless skies, and a minimum of fog, navigation becomes easy. Since that first sighting of the distant pack there had been no hint of ice and in fact this year there was no ice within a couple of hundred miles of Jan Mayen. It is not often thus. Had similar conditions prevailed in 1968 *Mischief* might be still afloat. Wishing to make our number to the Norwegians we headed for the small bay close to their base near the south-east end of the island, the bay of evil memory where *Mischief* had been so battered by the ice. It lies 4 miles up the east coast from Sorkapp and is a poor anchorage wide open to all winds from north-east round to south.

As Mike and I rowed ashore a small party gathered on the beach of black sand ready to give a hand hauling the dinghy clear of the surf. The English-speaking member of the reception committee shook hands with the remark; "Mr. Tilman, I presume." He had been at the base in 1968 and upon seeing another yellow-

hulled cutter in the bay had put two and two together and concluded that it was that man again. Over a glass of brandy and in-
numerable cups of coffee we learnt with disappointment that the
Danish party and my friend Dr. Jensen, the would-be chapattie-
maker, had already left the island. On the other hand, I was delighted to hear that with or without the aid of chapatties they had
succeeded in climbing Beerenberg, the great volcanic peak 7,677 ft.
high, ice from sea to summit, that dominates the island. At long
intervals the peak has been climbed by various parties and it was
recently in the news on account of renewed volcanic activity.
We found we could post letters, a plane visiting the island once
a month in summer, and we also collected a 40 lb. bag of flour
which we needed.

Next day we moved round to Kvalrossbukta, an anchorage on
the west coast. There are no safe or sheltered anchorages on Jan
Mayen but those on the west coast are preferable as that coast is
free from any off-lying dangers. On quitting the bay that morning
we ran into thick fog. We lay becalmed in this fog not much more
than a mile from the coast and the outlying rock pinnacle upon
which *Mischief* had struck in similar foggy conditions, I made
sure that history did not now repeat itself. Keep the danger in
sight is a sound maxim, so on hearing the melancholy sound of
breakers from where we thought Sorkapp lay we motored in that
direction and presently made out the loom of the cape. West
of the cape the fog lifted and we enjoyed a brisk sail up the coast
to Kvalrossbukta in bright evening sunshine. The Norwegians
have oil tanks there, the oil being piped across the island, which at
this point is only 2 miles wide. Besides a hut used by the Norwegians there are a few graves of earlier visitors, the names upon
the wooden crosses no longer decipherable. It is highly unlikely
that any are the graves of the seven Dutchmen who wintered hereabouts in 1633, the first men ever to winter on the island. The
island was first sighted in 1607 by Henry Hudson and in 1633
the Dutch whaling fleet left seven of their men there to observe
through the winter the prevailing conditions. They all died of
scurvy, the last, who kept a diary right up to the end, dying only
a week or so before the return of the whaling fleet in the spring.

The two Brians spent the next day walking over to the base to
post letters. We found a meagre spring where Mike and Dougal
employed themselves filling jerrycans and ferrying them off to the

ship. I rove a new peak halyard and a few days later had the mortification of seeing this brand new length of rope stranded at one of the upper blocks. Close and constant vigilance is needed to see that all ropes are running clear. Short splices will not render through blocks, and long splices, unless really expertly made, are apt to come adrift, so this meant reeving another 60 fathoms of rope. We carry a lot of spare rope and obviously we need to. That evening a Norwegian sealer anchored in the bay having brought out and dropped at the base a French expedition.

Prelude to Disaster

The time had now arrived for us to try our luck. Three hundred miles to the west lay Scoresby Sound and in a matter of a few days we should meet with success or failure. Although up here in summer the winds are generally light they most often have an easterly component and would be in our favour. Having last year's experience vividly in mind, when ice stopped us 60 miles out from the coast, I was prepared for the worst, but as we sailed on in bright, cloudless weather with not a vestige of ice in sight my hopes revived. Would it be a case of third time lucky?

Sailing along quietly one can hardly say we ran on with bated breath but that was how I felt as the hours went by and still no ice appeared ahead. At last on 3rd August when only some 10 miles off the entrance to the Sound we began meeting floes. They were well scattered and having found a suitable one—large, flat, straight-sided—we moored to it and passed a peaceful night. We had learnt the mooring technique in 1970 on the west coast where we had spent many days moored to floes. Besides the charm of novelty, if one wants to stay put for the night it saves the trouble of jilling about or heaving-to and drifting. Next morning, and not without strong hopes, we started motoring through scattered floes towards the Sound. For four hours or so, going slowly, we had no serious trouble and we must have been within a few miles of the settlement at C. Tobin on the northern side before the leads gradually became harder to find, narrower, and sometimes ending in a cul-de-sac. The view from the mast-head offered little comfort and regretfully I gave the word for retreat. It was high time. The day had clouded over and a freshening wind from the east had set up enough swell to start the floes rocking up and down in a way that made contact with them something to be avoided, while the business of mooring to one became difficult if not hazardous. If we were to spend the night among floes, mooring was preferable to heaving-to, because when hove-to we should be constantly drifting down on floes and having to let draw to get clear.

As we retraced our steps eastwards and the ice became more open none of the floes we passed quite answered our specification— a respectable size, somewhat bigger, say, than a tennis court, a straight sheer side against which to put our stem while the mooring party jumped ashore, and a few ice bollards or embryo humps which could be quickly fashioned into bollards with an ice-axe. While manœuvring close to one to assess its suitability our stern sustained a sufficiently hard knock to further cool my waning interest in mooring to a floe. Better to get out to sea clear of the ice. In the course of implementing this decision we passed a floe that looked more promising. It had no bollards ready made or even embryo bollards but a crack or miniature crevasse running across it seemed to be designed to hold a grapnel.

By this time the freshening wind and the swell that was running would have persuaded anyone less pig-headed to desist. We approached up wind and while I put her stem against a short stretch of clean-cut, steep-to ice Mike leapt off the bowsprit with the grapnel. By the time Mike had fixed the grapnel the wind had blown the boat's head to one side so that short of running off and making a fresh approach head to wind it was impossible to put her stem back against the steep-to edge. To save time and to make sure of recovering Mike I ran her forefoot up the sloping shelf of ice immediately ahead while Mike, an athletic chap, waded down the shelf, leapt for the bowsprit end, and swung himself up. We backed off the shelf readily enough then lay to the warp and grapnel. We soon realised that we had wasted our time. The floe was not massive enough to lie immovable. More floes drifted down, joggled against it, and started it spinning slowly round until after a couple of uneasy hours the grapnel pulled out of the crack. Recovering both warp and grapnel intact we went out to sea for the night.

For the next few days we jilled about in the offing, greatly encouraged by the rapid disappearance of all the ice outside the Sound. From C. Tobin, off which we lay, for 17 miles south to C. Brewster the sea was clear of ice while the Sound itself remained chock-a-block with ice, mixed with great icebergs. Meantime, away to the south, unknown to us, a small vessel that was, however, a great deal more powerful than *Seabreeze*, after a battle with the ice, successfully penetrated the Sound. The skipper of this vessel, then engaged in geodetic survey, was a friend of mine from whom I subsequently had the following letter. They had sailed for Scoresby Sound from Angmagssalik on 3rd August.

On the way to Scoresby Sound we were forced by ice to go east and at one time were not more than forty miles from Iceland. From there we went direct to Scoresby Sound but at the entrance were stopped by heavy, close packed ice, and were beset for twelve hours near C. Brewster. We got in a bad position and could not move and during this time five big bergs were forced out of the Sound by under-currents. One of them passed our ship only 15 ft. away with a huge forefoot underneath us. When the bergs had passed the ice slackened a little and we were able to make our way behind C. Brewster where we found a shore lead two miles wide along the coast to C. Stevenson. From there we found the area nearly free from ice. We stayed for a week and had excellent weather. The ice we forced was heavy and too much for a ship like yours not ice protected.

In this letter Captain Toft makes no mention of having crossed the Sound to the settlement at C. Tobin so what the ice thereabouts may have been like remains unknown. Had we but known beforehand of this visit we might have cruised off C. Brewster instead of C. Tobin and so fallen in with Captain Toft. Meeting him would have been fun. On the other hand we might have been tempted to follow his powerful ship through the ice with unfortunate results. We had tried that several years before in *Mischief* off Angmagssalik and had got ourselves into trouble with complete success.

For want of better our only plan at the moment was to wait and see whether the ice would move out of the Sound. Just as patience is a virtue easily fatigued by exercise, so waiting about at sea in a small boat is a tiring game to play. One thought of the blockading ships in Nelson's day lying off some French or Spanish port for months on end in fair weather or foul. But they were under orders and not on a pleasure cruise, and they were buoyed up, too, by the prospect of imminent action or of prizes to be taken. Some islands a few miles north of C. Tobin offered a chance of finding an anchorage but having gone there we found the ice lying thick jammed between the islands and the coast. Our hopes were similarly dashed when we inspected a bay just outside the Sound close to C. Tobin where there were a few Greenlander houses. There, a belt of shore-fast ice extended out for several hundred yards, and this was the more frustrating because we could now see the wireless masts of the settlement sticking up from behind the cape only a few miles away.

The engine in *Seabreeze* was a two-cylinder Kermath "Hercules", an American engine, installed in 1958. Apart from a reluctance to start from cold it had given no trouble since I had had the boat. In these cold waters we made a point of starting it every two or three days, and if it had not been in use would run it for an hour to keep the batteries charged. On 8th August, a black day in the annals of *Seabreeze*, it made a queer noise when started and on being stopped refused to start again. I remembered 8th August because on that day in 1969, with C. Brewster in sight, the crew had refused to go on. (Incidentally 8th August was what Hindenberg called the German army's "black day" on account of the successful British attack at Amiens in 1918 when I happened to be serving as a subaltern in "I" troop R.H.A.) Various were the suggestions made but no one among the crew could diagnose the fault, much less cure it. Colin Putt, the maestro in these matters, believes the trouble to have been a broken valve spring and had he been with us perhaps the engine could have been run on one cylinder.

Later that day, various remedies having been tried in vain, we reluctantly concluded that the engine had "had it". From then on we were a sailing ship in the strict sense of the word and a more prudent man might have taken this as a hint that it was time to quit the coast of Greeenland where, without an engine, or even with one, it is easy for a small boat to find itself in trouble. No waters are foolproof and Arctic waters are less so than any. Before the days of engines ships that plied their trade in the Arctic were built for the job and usually cruised in company so that if one was holed or nipped in the ice help was at hand. Anyhow, we would gain nothing now by waiting; ice conditions in the Sound might become easier but they would not become easy enough for us to manœuvre in without an engine. Before starting for home we needed water and stores, and instead of some Iceland port I thought we might get them at Angmagssalik, thus giving the crew the slight satisfaction of having set foot in Greenland. The entrance to Angmagssalik is narrow but quite wide enough to sail through if unencumbered by ice, and I reckoned that by the time we got there, say about 20th August, there would be little of that left.

The fact that the ice seemed to be confined to the Sound, the offing remaining more or less ice-free, led me to suppose that the coast to the south would be equally free. The prospect of sailing south, helped by the east Greenland current, keeping this magnificently mountainous coast close aboard all the way to Angmagssalik gave me great pleasure. How wrong can one be. A few miles south of C. Brewster we began meeting ice and the further south we went and the further from the coast—for the coast trends south-west—the more we met. When a large field of ice appeared on our port hand to the east we had something to worry about, for by holding on southwards we might find ourselves embayed. We went about and sailed north again until with open water to the east we could safely sail in that direction. It proved a slow passage and not without some alarms.

A long way from Greenland and in fact within 70 miles of Iceland, we were not expecting to meet any ice when in the darkest hours of a foggy night we found ourselves sailing among scattered floes. These were evidently the remnants of the pack that we had seen in the distance on the way to Jan Mayen three weeks before. We hove-to until daylight and then had to sail further east to win clear, and what with this and contrary winds we had Iceland once more in sight before we were able to head west for the passage across Denmark Strait. One might almost think that a watchful Providence was trying to keep us away from Greenland. There were a surprising number of icebergs roaming widely over Denmark Strait, even within sight of Iceland, for it is not usual to meet them so far away from the Greenland coast.

On the night of 19th August, when only some thirty to forty miles east of C. Dan, we encountered a hard north-easterly gale, quite the hardest blow of the voyage and one which went on for twenty-four hours. We had sea-room enough, for at C. Dan the coast falls away to the west, and we needed it as we drifted away to the south-west, hove-to and with only some six feet of the luff hoisted. On the morning of the 21st, the gale being then spent, we had land in sight to the north, but a heavy bank of fog lay over the sea, only the mountains showing above it, and it was impossible to identify anything. In the distance there was a ship evidently making for Angmagssalik and presently a Norwegian whaler appeared out of the fog and closed with us for a gam. He had been sheltering in Angmagssalik during the gale and was now on the way out to sea seeking.

One of the crew spoke a little English but we had difficulty in making ourselves understood. We told them of our engine trouble and finally managed to get from them what we wanted which was the course and distance to Angmagssalik—15 miles north-west. They then sheered off into the fog but presently we heard his engines again and once more he ranged alongside. They said they had spoken to Angmagssalik radio station and had been told in return that we would be helped in. We had not asked for a tow nor did I think it likely, in spite of what the Norwegians said, that anyone at Angmagssalik would bother their heads about us. On the other hand I felt pretty confident that if we did meet a local vessel near the entrance a tow would be forthcoming if we needed one—especially if the local vessel happened to be *Ejnar Mikelsen*, for example, whose skipper was an old friend. Later on we were to hear what the reaction had been to this friendly effort on our behalf by the Norwegian whaler.

The fog slowly dispersed and by evening we had closed the land a few miles south of Angmagssalik, a narrow belt of ice-floes ahead and beyond that open water and a rocky shore. The wind was light and what little there was unfavourable and I had half made up my mind to spend the night at sea. However, when an opening appeared in the thin line of floes ahead I decided to sail through and try to find an anchorage for the night in Sermilik fjord which lay temptingly wide and open to the south-west, a fateful decision that was to have consequences. This was an error of judgement. Sermilik is one of the fjords that has at its head a large glacier descending from the inland ice so that there is a constant supply of ice lurking somewhere in the fjord. Still there was little enough in sight at the moment and even if we failed to find an anchorage we were not likely to come to harm, the weather apparently settled and the glass still rising after the recent gale. Having sailed through the belt of floes without hitting any of them very hard and having reached open water, I felt satisfied. After more than three weeks at sea it would be pleasant to be at anchor in a Greenland fjord even though it was not in Scoresby Sound.

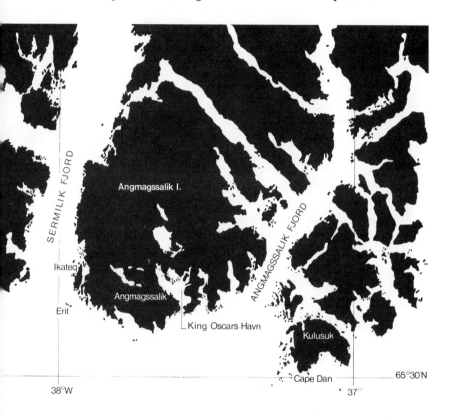

CHAPTER EIGHT

Wreck of "Seabreeze"

The wind became fluky and finally died when we were still a mile or more from the shore. We tried towing with the dinghy without success, nor were we so well equipped with oars and planks as on the previous voyage. A couple of long sweeps would have done the business. The glass had been rising smartly and was now high, the more unexpected therefore was the fierce onset of wind that came in suddenly from the north just as darkness fell, the herald of a dirty night. The first blast laid her over until the lee deck was half under water. The boat shot ahead, rapidly closing the dimly seen shore. She had way enough on, I reckoned, to take her in, and the rate we were going and the fear that we might hit something induced me to get the sails off in a hurry. I had misjudged the distance and we could get no bottom with the lead.

By this time the wind or the tide had brought quantities of ice down the fjord. Increasing numbers of floes were spinning by, so many that the thought of rehoisting and trying to sail among them in the dark with that strength of wind was too daunting. In fact all hands had their work cut out fending off the floes. The dinghy was still lying astern and we had no hands to spare to hoist it on board. For the next two or three hours we drifted slowly across the mouth of the fjord until some rock skerries loomed out of the darkness to leeward. In an effort to sail clear we got the stays'l up and we might have succeeded had not a floe got under the lee bow and stopped her. Her heel caught on a ledge and she spun round to be pinned by wind and waves against the rock, the cranse iron at the bowsprit end striking sparks from the rock face as she plunged in the surge. Dropping the stays'l we shoved desperately and vainly to get her off. She was hard and fast and taking a terrible hammering as she rose and fell on the

6. "Picturesque" berg, while 7 (*below*) shows a block berg which has five times as much ice under water.

8. Weathered berg in Umanak Fjord. *Photo: Ilan Rosengarten*

ledge. Fearing she would soon break up or slip off the ledge into deep water I told the crew to take what gear they could and to abandon ship by jumping for the rock.

Waves swept the ledge on which she lay but from the ledge dry land was within easy reach. A sack of hastily collected food was first thrown ashore followed by Mike who took with him a line which he anchored to a boulder. Young Dougal then tied himself on and got ashore safely, though the line would have been better secured on board to use as a handrail. Without waiting for Mike to coil and throw back the rope Brian, the cook, clambered over the side and jumped for the ledge. A wave caught him and washed him back almost under the boat before the next wave took him shorewards to be grabbed by Mike and hauled to safety wet through from head to foot. The wind, the breaking waves, and the crashing noise made by the boat as she pounded prevented any communication with those on shore who still had both ends of the line. The lead line being the only rope handy young Brian tied himself to that and jumped while I held him. This left me with the weighted end and thinking, rather stupidly, that 7 lb. of lead round the waist might be a hindrance if it came to swimming I had to go below for a knife to cut the lead off. Normally I wear a knife on my belt and to be without one then was unseamanlike, as indeed was much of our behaviour that night.

Total darkness reigned below. Nor could I find a torch. But after first being thrown violently to the floor with a crash that made me think the deck had caved in I found my knife, regained the deck, and presently joined the others, wet only from the waist down. I am ashamed to confess that from our first striking, while all this was happening, it never even occurred to me to collect such essential and easily portable things as diary, log book, films, money, or sextant, all of which could have been stuffed in a rucksack and got ashore. As Dr. Johnson well says:

> . . . how often a man that has pleased himself at home with his own resolution, will, in the hour of darkness and fatigue, be content to leave behind everything but himself.

We moved a few yards inland to seek shelter under a low rock wall from the wind and from the rain that had now set in. I found I could not walk without support, the ground seeming to go up and down as it sometimes does on first landing after a rough passage. On taking stock our position seemed to be grimmer than it need have been. We were all wet, some wetter than others. All had sleeping bags but precious little else. Mike had done best by bringing a very light bivouac tent. I had a tin of tobacco, a dry box of matches, but no pipe. Brian, who had not spent the night on deck like the rest of us, had no oilskins and wore carpet slippers instead of gumboots. On the other hand he had a wet and useless camera. No one had brought any food and the sack that had been first thrown ashore had been washed away.

It was then about 1 a.m. and after a couple of hours of fitful dozing, at the first hint of dawn, some of us got up and went down to the wreck. By then I had recovered my balance. Only the top of the mast showed above water. She had evidently filled and slipped off the ledge, but whether this had happened soon after our leaving or later we could not tell. Even had there been time it would have been difficult and indeed perilous to go back on board to retrieve anything. Jumping down and getting ashore was one thing, but it would have been quite another to maintain a footing on the wave-swept ledge near enough to the boat to grab something and climb up her heaving side.

At full light we moved up to the top of our rock islet which was, I suppose, some seventy or eighty feet high and nearly a hundred yards across. On the chart it is called Erit. There we pitched the bivouac tent and Brian and Dougal, who were wettest and coldest, were put inside. We other three explored every nook and cranny of the rock, finding it rich in nothing but pools of rain-water. At least we should not die of thirst. Returning to the scene of the wreck we searched vainly for flotsam, or even for the jetsam we had thrown overboard—the sack of food. I examined closely a narrow crack full of brash ice. Among the ice was a piece of white board from the after hatch and, Heaven be praised, a pipe, one of several that I had on board. That was all that came ashore.

After this lucky find, there being no interlude for breakfast, Mike, young Brian, and I, spent the morning pacing up and down, scanning the sea (empty except for ice), and speculating on our future. The nearest shore of the fjord was about 2 miles away. Brian's suggestion for paddling across on an ice floe seemed fraught with difficulties, not least the lack of paddles. Out of sight and a few miles up the fjord there was, as I knew, a small settlement, Ikateq, and no doubt there would be communication by boat between this and Angmagssalik. How frequently or infrequently was the question; and supposing a vessel of some kind did pass, would we be seen? We had no flares and no means of making smoke except by burning the tent or somebody's gumboots. Once a week, I thought, might be a reasonable guess, and we ought to be able to keep alive for that long. Perhaps if the sun had been shining and our clothes getting drier instead of wetter, for it was still raining, the prospect of a week or so without food might have been less daunting. Some might consider fasting no hardship, indeed beneficial. As Mr. Pecksniff said: "If everyone were warm and well-fed we should lose the satisfaction of admiring the fortitude with which others bear cold and hunger."

After lunch—one gets into the habit of so apportioning the day— or say, two o'clock we tried squeezing three into the tent where it was warmer than outside but no drier. Young Brian took the first spell and an hour later I began crawling in for my turn. At that moment Mike let out a yell, "A boat". There had already been one false alarm and I expected this too would turn out to be an ice floe. But there was no mistake. Close to the north shore and bound up the fjord was one of the small, local boats with the familiar red hull. At that distance, on a dull, drizzling afternoon, I doubted if they would spot us. All five of us gathered on the highest point of the rock and began waving our sleeping bags. Some even started shouting, futile enough considering the distance and the fact that her Greenlander crew would be sensibly and drily ensconsed in their wheelhouse.

To our dismay she held steadily on course and we thought bitterly how stupid they must be to fail to notice five men standing on top of an uninhabited skerry. Or perhaps they mistook the flapping figures for those grotesque and frightening mythological creatures depicted in Eskimo carvings, known as *tubilaks*, and had wisely decided to give Erit a wide berth. We had about given up hope when the boat slowed and turned in our direction. They had seen us all right as one might have known they would. No Greenlander worth his salt could fail to see us. Besides being keen-eyed they have an abiding interest in seals or anything shootable and while on passage, however routine it may be, are always on the alert and keeping a good look-out.

The crew of three set about the rescue in a seamanlike way. While the boat lay-to they launched a capacious dinghy which two of them brought close in to the rock stern-to, taking us all off in turn without mishap. Below in the cuddy they had an oil stove roaring away and relays of hot coffee were soon produced. Meantime the boat continued up the fjord to Ikateq where there were forty drums of oil—the winter fuel supply—to be landed. The crew of *Seabreeze* lent a willing hand, young Brian in the hold slinging the drums, Dougal on the derrick guy, with Mike and Brian on the beach man-handling the landed drums. I was thankful when Brian and the last drum emerged from the hold, for the wire sling was so badly stranded that the most careless stevedore would have condemned it at sight.

Halfway to Angmagssalik we were met and taken on board a far superior vessel, one used by the doctor for visits to outlying settlements. On board were the doctor himself and the head of the Angmagssalik police force. We disappointed the doctor in that we needed no treatment but we were able to reassure the policeman who was a worried man. News travels too fast nowadays. The Danish naval authorities on the west coast had already heard of our rescue and were asking how and why *Seabreeze* had come to grief. Apparently the message from the Norwegian whaler had been passed to the policeman who in turn had consulted the Harbour-master as to whether anything should be done. His opinion had been that since a tow would cost £200, and that since from the Norwegian's unflattering description we were not likely to have that amount even in pennies, nothing should be done. Since we had neither asked for a tow nor expected one the policeman had no cause for worry.

We spent that night in the hospital where we were given a room to ourselves and most kindly looked after. Next day I had to give a full account of the stranding to our policeman, with my friend, the skipper of *Ejnar Mikelsen*, acting as interpreter. The head of the Administration was in a hurry to get rid of us. A Danish ship about to sail had only two vacant berths and since none of the crew had any money or passports we had to travel together. The quickest and cheapest alternative was to charter a small plane from Reykjavik and we arranged to be picked up next day which was a Friday. Near C. Dan, on the island of Kulusuk, there is an airstrip. Money proved to be no problem, the Administrator, acting for the Danish Government, being delighted to lend me as many thousands of kroner as I needed, on note of hand alone as the money-lenders say. Leaving the hospital we messed and slept that night in the huts used by the Danish technicians and workmen who in summer are employed in Greenland.

Early on the Friday we again embarked in the doctor's boat for passage to Kulusuk, a matter of about an hour and a half. In dense fog and with large numbers of bergs and floes about the skipper made full use of his radar. The harbour at Kulusuk, too, was cluttered with floes and a U.S. naval transport lying there looked uncommonly forlorn in those bleak surroundings. Fog persisted throughout the day and on the last of my several visits to the control tower they told me there would be no flight that day. This was awkward, since it meant our arriving at Reykjavik on the Saturday when the bank to which I had had money for our fares home sent would be shut. Taking my family home was proving expensive enough without having to spend the week-end in a Reykjavik hotel. There is a pretty large staff at Kulusuk (it is part of the Early Warning System) so we ate in their mess and were given rooms in a hostel (all on payment) used by visitors and passengers in transit.

Our plane, a five-seater Apache, arrived next day at noon and after lunch we embarked. Our luggage hardly needed weighing and slight though it was we had a job stuffing it in. Our pilot, long-haired, nonchalant, extremely youthful, a cigarette dangling from his lips, did not inspire confidence. This, together with my reinforced mistrust of engines, made me, if not apprehensive, yet looking forward with some eagerness to a safe landing on the far side of Denmark Strait. I need not have worried. The manager of the charter company, who did a lot for us later at Reykjavik, assured me that he was the best pilot they had ever had.

Late that evening we reached Reykjavik where happily the British Consul had got wind of us. I had met him before in Reykjavik in 1965, and the manager of the charter company now drove me to his office where we were fixed up with a bit of paper that served as a passport for the whole crew and seats on a flight to London next day, for which the Consul paid. The manager of the charter company kindly allowed us to bed down in the top storey of his office in a room that originally had been the airfield control tower. Although we arrived in London a day later than I had indicated we were met and shepherded through the formalities by a relative of mine, Brigadier Davis, accompanied by Bob

Comlay. No one having been drowned the loss of *Seabreeze* happily escaped publicity, but an ITV man lying in wait sought an interview with the persistence of the importunate widow until some rude words from Bob Comlay silenced him. Colin Putt, too, just missed us but came along next morning to drive me to Wales.

At the moment there are few if any amateur sailors likely to profit by it, but for me the lesson of this sad story is not to mess about in Greenland fjords without an engine, especially when they are full of ice. For all that I feel we were victims of an unlucky chain of circumstance—the calm that prevented us from finding an anchorage, followed shortly by a wind of such force that we could not sail safely among the ice brought down by the wind, but for which we would have come to no harm. *Seabreeze* had made four voyages north and each voyage had seen some small improvement introduced. At the end I felt as proud and confident of her as I had of *Mischief* and thought her to be as able a boat as on the day of her launching in 1899. The fact that she had on her last voyage a new boom and a new mainsail was merely another trifling sum of misery added to the account. Certainly a staggering enough blow for me and only the fact that we had not sailed the seas so long nor had so many adventures together made her loss a little less heart-rending than that of *Mischief*. For fourteen years *Mischief* and I had sailed together and at the end I had to watch helpless while she lay on the beach, so battered by sea and ice that she did not long survive when finally got under tow.

Concerning regrettable incidents, and this ranks as such, Sir Winston Churchill's advice was never to look back, look to the future. Such advice is easier to give than to take, but in a case like mine it would help if I had another boat. Within a short time of getting home I heard of a boat that was to be sold in November, and having had a look at her I felt that, all being well, the future was arranged. When in October I learnt that she was not going to be sold I had to think again and these thoughts led back to *Seabreeze* and the possibility of raising her. I kicked myself for not having stopped in Reykjavik on the way home to make enquiries, but that had not been possible as I had to take the crew home. There were no facilities at Angmagssalik, if anything were to be done it would be from Reykjavik.

From Lloyds I obtained the name of a firm in Reykjavik to

whom I wrote. They thought it a wild idea, a moonbeam from a larger lunacy, but were extremely helpful. Even if it could be done, they said, the cost of salvage and repair would be out of proportion to the value of the ship, and in any case, before approaching a salvage company the wreck would have to be examined by a diver. They reckoned that a diver could be flown to Kulusuk and taken by boat to the wreck for about £550, given favourable conditions. This preliminary stake, which would probably be lost anyway, seemed to me to be worth putting down. I felt I owed it to *Seabreeze* to make an effort, and the diver, besides reporting on the state of the wreck, might with a little encouragement be persuaded to retrieve a few valuables. I had in mind particularly a couple of sextants and £70 in Danish money.

All this took time and clearance had to be got from Copenhagen. But at length Messrs. Könun, the agents, laid on a diver and a charter flight for him and me for 15th November. On this I booked a flight to Reykjavik and for the second time had money transferred to a bank there. The day before I was due to go the following cable came from Messrs. Könun who, by the way, were not sparing of words either in their letters or their cables:

> We have today received following from airfield manager Kulusuk in reply to our queries. Regarding *Seabreeze* stop undersigned plus helicopter crew ascertained 28th October from helicopter in spite of clear water and visible bottom no sign of *Seabreeze* stop it is assumed that the wreck has been washed away during heavy storms regards manager Kulusuk. In view of this information which must be relied upon we do not consider it in your interest to send diver stop.

At first I thought there was something fishy about this, even that the airfield manager had an eye to salvaging the boat himself and did not want a visit from me. Accordingly I asked Messrs. Könun why he had bothered to fly a helicopter over the wreck on 28th October and how did he know where to look. To which they replied that the wreck had been observed in about 30 metres of water several times from both speed-boats and helicopter; which implied that she was already in deeper water than when we left her with her mast showing, and that by 28th October she had gone deeper still and out of sight. In their reply they added a suggestion from the airfield manager that if I wanted to look for myself I could hire a helicopter for £250 an hour.

I had to withdraw my suspicions about the airfield manager and after much heart-searching decided to throw in my hand. The approach of winter was a decisive factor. If the wreck were located, if the diver succeeded in reaching it, and if he reported favourably —three big "ifs"—nothing could be done until the next summer, by which time the wreck might have slipped further down. I consulted my friend Captain Toft who wrote: "I am sure it is quite impossible to find *Seabreeze* now because of drifting ice, strong tides, and deep water close to shore. Any money spent on a search has to be lost money." Another Danish skipper also wrote to me: "I think there is a deep round Erit and *Seabreeze* has slid down to the foot of the islet, so I think you are right to forget her and look for another ship. It will be too expensive to raise the yacht and get her repaired. A wooden ship will get very severe damage when hammered on rock broadside on."

I now had to reproach myself for not having done something early in September when at least the boat might have been found and examined, and to regret that the prospect of acquiring another boat had led to neglecting the slight chance of saving my old one. Thus having muffed both possibilities I had to bestir myself if I were not to be left high and dry with no voyage in view for 1973. I will not say that the idea of giving up, calling it a day had not occurred to me, but I regarded this as the prompting of Belial who "with words clothed in reason's garb, counselled ignoble ease". We hear sad stories of men retiring after a life of toil and trouble who instead of enjoying their well-earned ease and freedom from care find it so insupportable that they soon fall into a decline. No doubt a friend, evidently a classical scholar, had this in mind when he sent me the following snippet of ancient wisdom: "The man who would be fully employed should procure a ship or a woman, for no two things produce more trouble" (Plautus 254–184 B.C.). The year ended on a happier note with a promise of full employment and a stock of trouble. *Baroque*, a Pilot cutter of 1902 vintage, was for sale, and needless to say I bought her.

CHAPTER NINE

"Baroque"

One cannot buy a biggish boat as if buying a piece of soap. The act is almost as irrevocable as marriage and should be given as much thought. Even if the boat is bought merely to look at, as some are, it has to lie somewhere. Expenses begin at once and if the boat is an old one they will rise in arithmetical progression until either something happens to it or the owner finds himself in Carey Street. When I first heard of *Baroque* she was lying at Mylor near Falmouth and early in January 1973 I went down there. Mylor is in the uttermost parts of the West, as the Psalmist has it, though to me, driving from North Wales in winter, it seemed like the uttermost part of the earth. On this first reconnaissance I broke the journey, but on subsequent visits did the 350-odd miles in the day, straightening one's back with difficulty at the end of it and continuing to vibrate for several hours afterwards.

Baroque measured 50 ft. overall, 13 ft. 6 ins. beam, 7 ft. 6 ins. draught, and 32 tons T.M.; thus she was a foot longer than *Seabreeze* and a foot less in beam. She lay against the harbour wall, drying out at low tide, and at first sight the doghouse that some misguided person had stuck on her, and the tall pole mast, rather put me off. Pilot cutters should have flush decks or at worst low skylights, so the doghouse was incongruous and spoilt her looks. The tall pole mast was in keeping, but it meant extra gear and weight aloft without much gain. The occasions on which one would want to set a tops'l in the North Atlantic are so few that such a sail is hardly worth carrying. Both *Seabreeze* and *Mischief* had topmasts that could be lowered or dispensed with altogether, as in the end they were. *Baroque*'s upper and lower backstays were lavishly lapped with baggywrinkle, lending her a picturesque appearance and adding weight and windage to the stays. This stuff, easily made up from strands of old rope, preserves the mains'l from chafe. Normally, however, the lee backstays would be cast off and secured by the shrouds so that the wire stay would seldom be against the sail. Probably previous owners had used her mainly for day-sailing and were content to ease away the lee backstays without casting them off altogether as would be done on a long passage. She had been built in 1902 and since her working days had suffered at the hands of various owners all with various ideas, most of them wrong.

It is time to go below and at the risk of being tedious I ought to describe what I found and my reactions, which were those of a man who has already half made up his mind to commit a folly and is already thinking of ways to mitigate it. Starting at the forward end the peak was roomy—a sail rack would have to be built in. Nor was there any chain locker and no chute for the chain to be led down from the winch. In fact she had no substantial ground tackle at all, only a little Fisherman type anchor suitable for a dinghy and a CQR anchor of about 20 lbs. with a few fathoms of $\frac{1}{4}$ in. chain. On the other hand she had a fine, big winch. A chain locker and chain chute would therefore have to be made, while a Fisherman anchor of about 1 cwt., a 60 lbs. CQR, and some 35 fathoms of $\frac{1}{2}$ in. chain would have to be bought. This want of ground tackle, and the absence or flimsiness of various fittings, confirmed that if she had been sailed at all it had been as a day-boat, a day's sail and back to a mooring. Cleats were scarce and small, there were no sheet-leads for either jib or stays'l, and the compass was a small plastic affair mounted on a bakelite bracket screwed to thin plywood.

Abaft the peak came the galley, sink with taps, gas cooker and refrigerator. All would have to be abolished. So far forward the motion is felt most and it would be a long walk carrying food from the galley to the saloon. Instead of the sink I could have a work bench with vice and there would be room, too, for a huge locker with five shelves big enough to hold all our stores. A bunk occupied the port side and a ladder and forehatch gave access to the deck; the presence of the hatch led one to suspect that this bunk might prove to be wet. The art of making watertight hatches has not yet been perfected.

A bulkhead separated this from the next compartment aft which had two bunks to port and one to starboard. Aft of the two bunks a sliding door led into the "heads". The mast came down aft of the bulkhead and overhead was a small skylight. The galley would have to go here, the two bunks being sacrificed in favour of a sink with shelves below and above. The proximity of the galley to the lavatory might not please a sanitary inspector but that could not be helped. This sliding door, by the way, soon gave up sliding and had to be abolished like all the other doors, the only door left being that between the chartroom and the cockpit. The throne in the "heads" had been built for someone with abnormally long legs. We had to put in a foot-rest. At one end of this small compartment a shower had been installed. Pipes writhed everywhere, a Laocoon coil of them, hot water and cold, salt water and fresh. The plumber, not one of the brightest, had a job sorting them out and sealing off the unwanted majority.

Next came the saloon or main cabin, very ornate with mahogany panelling, red baize inside the panels, gimballed brass lamps looking like old-fashioned oil lamps but in fact electric, the whole spacious enough but nowhere to put anything and no table. Brian Potter, cook on the previous voyage, who later came down to lend a hand with *Baroque*, thought that these gimballed lamps (a dozen of them) would be of value to antique dealers. The dealers thought otherwise so Brian converted them back to oil for use in *Baroque*. The two settee berths in the saloon had under them little locker space and only meagre cupboards for the occupants' kit. In fact, in spite of her size there seemed to be little room to stow anything. By putting another bunk over the one on the port side I could have five bunks, the number required, and there remained only the table problem. In *Mischief* we had a 100-gallon water tank in the saloon with a table on top and the same could be done here; owing to the shape of the hull the final result was a tank of only 60 gallons, leaving just enough room for a passageway on one side and barely enough room to sit at the table on the other.

Two steps led from the saloon up into the combined chartroom and engineroom comprising the doghouse, standing a good four feet above deck level, made of plywood, and large perspex windows all round. Apart from its ugliness it was a source of weakness, but nothing much could be done. A wave might abolish it but I could not very well abolish it myself since it housed the engine, and without it there would be nowhere to do any chart-work. The main water tank of 60 gallons lay underneath with a 40-gallon

75

header-tank to one side. Here, too, were the fuel tanks winged out on either side. These were two 40-gallon oil drums, effective enough, one supposed, until they rusted through. The charging motor for the batteries, which were also housed here, was a portable Honda. The engine, a Ford diesel marine conversion, looked huge and lurked below floor level on the port side with a lot of vacant space round it.

Aft of the doghouse was a deep and narrow cockpit, lockers either side and a big locker under the seat. The helmsman had to stand on the seat in order to see over the doghouse roof; in the end we had to add something more to stand on so that he could see enough. Steering was by wheel with a not over-robust looking worm gear and this, too, would need to be abolished in favour of a tiller with less to go wrong and more positive action. Except for the bowsprit the spars looked in good condition, while the sails, which were almost new, were of terylene with not very stout stitching. This certainly has the no mean advantage of being light, easy to hoist and handle, easy to stow, and stowable when wet without fear of rot. On the whole, however, I would still prefer heavy canvas, if only as more in keeping with an old boat. It would be a better bet, too, in tropical waters since terylene does not stand up well to prolonged sunshine. Except for the bowsprit shrouds the wire standing rigging was in good shape. The shrouds were attached to the chain plates with rigging screws, whereas I would have preferred lanyards like we had in *Seabreeze*. These again are more in keeping with a boat built in 1902 and having more give are possibly less cruel to the hull. The chain plates looked short.

> Be to her faults a little blind
> And to her virtues ever kind

is advice equally applicable when proposing to throw in one's lot with either a woman, a horse, or a boat. *Baroque* might have virtues and some of her more obvious faults could be corrected, if not ignored. At that late stage, January, if I were to have a cruise that summer it would have to be in *Baroque*, for there was no other boat in sight. Much needed to be done but nothing like so much as we had had to do with *Seabreeze*, and she could probably be got ready by the end of May. A cruise to northern waters every summer had become almost as essential as breathing, so strong is habit, and since in the natural course of things there could not be many more

I did not want to leave 1973 blank; if a year were missed to start again would be all the harder. Another persuasive factor in *Baroque*'s favour was a specification I saw of work done to her in 1970 for her then owners. She had had then a major overhaul and they had spent a lot of money. As events were to show they had not spent nearly enough.

Or perhaps, as I presently discovered, the work had not been as thorough as it should have been. Even on this first visit I noticed that no new keel-band had been fitted as specified, the old one being still in place with a break in it. On a second visit made a week or so later to discuss terms with the owner, John Smith, who had owned the boat for only a few months, we made a worse discovery. Since my first visit he had on his own behalf taken out the gas cooker and the refrigerator thus exposing three or four frames on the starboard side. Two of these were rotten, without any fastenings, and could be waggled about by hand. I began to think I had been a bit hasty in making an offer. Thanks to a friend who lived in that rather lush region I got in touch with the owner of a nearby boatyard, Bob Pizey, extremely knowledgeable about old boats, who agreed to come over next day to do a quick survey.

The day started badly for Bob Pizey with an accident in his yard when a boat fell over and broke the leg of one of his men. In spite of that he came over to Mylor and devoted several hours to *Baroque*. Outside, the hull appeared to be in good condition, only one soft plank to be renewed and a short graving piece let into another. The propeller, shaft, and "A" bracket were corroded and needed renewing. The difficulties for a surveyor begin inside where, short of pulling the boat to pieces, he cannot see nearly as much as he would wish. On the other hand, in dealing with old boats, the more you stir the more it stinks. One needs to take a certain amount for granted, adopting the motto of the Australian opal-gouger, "Live in hope if you die in despair". We took out what mahogany panelling we could in order to inspect the frames behind and the nett result was two more rotten frames to add to the two already found. It might have been much worse and I made up my mind to go ahead, to buy the boat and to have the necessary work put in hand by the local yard.

On this brief visit to Mylor I acquired not only a boat but also the second of two prospective crew. Brian McClanaghan, not a whit discouraged by the disaster of the previous year, had already offered to come if I succeeded in finding a boat. This time I intended going first to west Greenland and then as far north as we could, a point that I hoped would turn out to be Ellesmere Island, the original objective in 1972. In an untried vessel, making as it were a trial voyage, this might seem ambitious; but to be of any value, to disclose defects and weaknesses, a trial voyage must be long enough to ensure experiencing a few gales. There are exceptions to this. On our first voyage in *Seabreeze*, for instance, the urgent need for re-caulking became apparent even before we had left the Solent.

My acquaintance with John Harradine, the second volunteer, had begun the previous year soon after the loss of *Seabreeze*, by his sending me a telegram in Latin, thus astonishing Barmouth Post Office and enhancing my bogus reputation as a man of learning. Latin is undoubtedly the right language for telegrams because one can say an awful lot in very few words. *O passi graviore revocate animos et haec olim meminisse juvabit* the telegram read, and with the help of a dictionary I translated this as "Ye who have suffered even greater trials gather courage, perhaps one day it will be pleasant to remember them." The sender gave no address and this had to be got with the aid of the Post Office sleuths. On our corresponding I found him keen on making a northern voyage and promised to let him know if I found a boat. In January he was in England on leave from Norway where he taught adult classes English, not Latin. I had told him of *Baroque* and of my impending second visit to Mylor.

The evening of the day when I had discovered the loose, rotten frames I was in the bar of the inn at Mylor Bridge, about 1½ miles from the harbour, in a very uncertain frame of mind and deriving neither aid nor comfort from the beer provided. A short, young man with reddish hair, wearing a duffel coat, walked in: "Mr. Tilman, I believe." This feat of detection impressed me. Mylor harbour and its vicinity is a maze of narrow roads leading in all directions, and to find his way from Watford to the boat and then in the dark of a January evening, guided only by his own resourcefulness, to run me to earth at Mylor Bridge showed him to be a man of determined enterprise. Neither the inn nor its beer encouraged conviviality. We had a quiet evening together while I explained the difficulties of my position and expressed the hope that by next afternoon as a result of Bob Pizey's survey I would know what to do. And just before closing time John Harradine supplied the last missing word for *The Times* crossword puzzle, a problem that had been worrying me all evening almost as much as the boat— an erudite man, as I had gathered from his telegram. As I had the only room in the inn John said he would go back and doss down in the boat. After he had left I remembered that the boat was locked up and that I had the key, but I did not think a trifle like that would baffle this resourceful man. In any case, "I'm all right, Jack," I thought, as I went up to my room, but on finding it extremely damp and chilly I was not so sure.

I had just finished my bacon and eggs when John, having slept in his van and breakfasted off a packet of biscuits, joined me and we adjourned to the boat to await Bob Pizey. Fortunately the tide was out and the hull accessible. We did a little more wrecking inside to expose more frames and on the whole the survey, as I have said, proved satisfactory. I decided to go ahead and John felt sufficient confidence in the boat to want to come on the projected voyage. He even went so far as to ask me to reserve the bunk forward of the galley for him, an unwise request.

CHAPTER TEN

Fitting Out and Crew

Mylor Yacht Harbour could now start on the work that I had planned, perforce hastily. The galley to be moved amidships and a work bench where the former galley had been; a big, new locker with five shelves to hold three or four months' food, a new bunk in the saloon, and water tank with table on top. (Owing to a strike on the part of galvanisers the tank had eventually to be made of fibre-glass.) A new bowsprit, chain plates for the topmast backstays (there were none), a wood tiller and an iron emergency tiller in lieu of the wheel. A Whale pump to be installed in addition to the semi-rotary; and new propeller, shaft, and "A" bracket. Later the stern tube was condemned as well and a new one had to be made. The ravages of electrolytic action seemed to be excessive, whether caused by Mylor sea-water or by the web of wiring, ancient and modern, which festooned *Baroque*'s interior. I should have liked to have done something with the doghouse either by removing or lowering it, but this meant an excessively expensive and time-consuming major upheaval. A radio telephone and an echo-sounder were part of her equipment. The latter had a fault which baffled the expert who spent two days trying to put it right. Regretfully I disposed of it. I had felt vaguely that we should fit one in *Mischief* and *Seabreeze* but had never done so, partly owing to a dislike of making more holes in the hull and partly from a mistrust of mechanical devices. The radio telephone, I learnt, could have been flogged for £200 had I owned the boat before 1st January when the enaction of some new regulations by the Post Office rendered it worthless. As already noted, the electric wiring needed simplifying. Like the water pipes, wires led everywhere, under the deck, along the deck, up the mast, under the cabin sole. We restricted the lighting to a binnacle light, and a light

9. Simon Richardson.

Photo: Ilan Rosengarten

10. *Baroque* leaving Mylor.

Photo: W. Stead

11. Skipper (*left*) and Brian McClanaghan in *Baroque*'s cabin

12. Beset in the ice.

in the doghouse, cabin, galley, and peak. With the water pipes,
as I have said, the plumber had a field day and lost. When we tried
the pump in the galley sink water came out where the shower
bath had been in the "heads".

The yard reckoned the work could be done by mid-May.
Sailing day had already been provisionally fixed for 29th May,
and I had now to complete the crew, a job that proved even more
tricky than usual. Even with a poor boat much can be achieved
by a good crew and since *Baroque* was an unknown quantity an
experienced and reliable crew was more desirable than ever.
Brian McClanaghan, his enthusiasm undiminished and his confidence unshaken by the loss of *Seabreeze*, knew the ropes and the
way things should be done, and was completely reliable. John
Harradine owned a small boat of his own so presumably knew
quite a bit, and he was also a mountaineer. An American who had
been recommended to me by a trusty friend thought he would
come and delayed until April to tell me that he would not. Early
in May he cabled to say that he had again changed his mind and
would join immediately, but this hardly merited the expense of
a reply. One or two other prospects faded out and by mid-April
the situation might have been described as desperate though not
hopeless. My letter to this effect to John Harradine who was back
in Norway, and who wanted to know the state of play, led to
embarrassing consequences—for him, at least, if not for me.

In the past an advertisement in *The Times* for "a cook for a cool
voyage" had been successful. Just before sending it for insertion
I noticed that someone else in reduced circumstances was advertis-
ing for "experienced crew for an Arctic voyage". My curiosity
roused I wrote to the Box Office number to enquire about his
voyage, at the same time asking the advertiser to let me have the
names and addresses of his rejects. He turned out to be Merton
Naydler whom I knew of as having sailed with David Lewis to
Iceland in a catamaran, subsequently writing a book called *Cook
in a Cool Cat*. He planned to sail to the Murmansk peninsula,
an objective that seemed to me to lack not only the prime requisites
of an Arctic voyage, namely ice and icebergs, but also to involve
the likelihood of having one's boat confiscated and ending up
in Lubalanka gaol. His rejected replies, he told me, had already
gone into the waste-paper basket but his secretary luckily re-
trieved them and passed them to me. I wrote to one or two that

sounded likely and later found that I had picked a winner in one, Simon Richardson, active, energetic, knowledgeable about boats and engines, and a thorough seaman so far as an amateur sailor can attain to that honourable title.

My own advertisement for cook produced fewer replies than expected, only eight in fact, the number having decreased steadily over the years. Whether this decrease implies a weakening of moral fibre on the part of the young or on the contrary a strengthening of the mind, only the sociologists would be likely to know. All eight very wisely asked for more details about the proposed voyage and on these being supplied all faded out except Ilan Rosengarten, another Australian in England on a working holiday. We exchanged several letters without getting any further and I had the impression that he had by no means made up his mind whether or not he wanted to come. By this time, early May, I was at Mylor living on board and starting to fit out. In fact I spent most of the time in Falmouth, Newlyn, and other places in search of the thousand and one things we needed. For the third time I was starting from scratch to collect what is necessary for a well-found ship and finding it uphill work.

Brian had arranged to join by 7th May, while John Harradine, who had talked of joining by Easter, was still in Norway. For the first week-end Colin Putt and Brian Potter, both highly skilled, came down to lend a hand, and having accomplished a lot in a short time left me in a more robust frame of mind, a little less daunted by the amount of gear still to be got and work to be done. The same week-end Simon Richardson and a friend of his came to see me and the boat, having spent the night, I gathered, in a tent on Bodmin Moor. I agreed to take Simon and thought there might be a berth for his friend as well if Ilan Rosengarten proved to be a non-starter. My last letter to Ilan had suggested his coming to Mylor to take stock of me and the boat if he was really interested; to my surprise he came. He did not tell me much about himself except that he was presently teaching in London and had not the least knowledge of boats, the sea, or expeditions. On the way back to Truro, where I took him to catch his train, I had to make up my mind, and it was with some misgiving that I finally told him to join. These misgivings were mainly owing to his total ignorance of boats and the sea, the difference, for instance, between cooking on a firmly based electric stove and on a most unstable Primus stove. Selfishly, I felt less concern for Ilan's prospects than those of the crew who would be put to some inconvenience or worse if we found our cook unable to cope.

As it happened, Ilan proved to be one of the best cooks I've ever had, either as regards cooking, housekeeping, or as shipmate. I take no credit for this. I had not, merely from his appearance, judged him to be willing, even-tempered, imperturbable, a man eager to overcome difficulties and able to rise to any occasion. I have long since given up trying to assess a man's character by his appearance or his behaviour at a brief interview, and in consequence of numerous errors of judgement have often lamented, like the hapless Duncan, that:

> There's no art
> To find the mind's construction in the face.

The fact is that it is easy to pick a winner when there is only one in the race, as was the case when Ilan came to Mylor to see me. For the first ten days or more my earlier misgivings looked like being justified for Ilan was far from well and took a long time to settle down. Having once recovered he never looked back and readily adapted himself to a strange way of life. He flavoured his cooking with imagination, always trying something new, and always busy in the galley except when beating me at chess. He served all meals on time whatever the weather, kept a close eye on water and stores, took a spell at the tiller when needed, and got on well with the crew. All ills are alleviated when attended by food and since the ills of this voyage were many we had frequent occasion to bless the cook.

With the arrival of Simon and Brian things began to move and I could look forward to more help from Colin Putt and Brian Potter who had promised to come down again before we sailed. The latter, with the experience of two voyages in the galley behind him, would impart some of this know-how to Ilan and start him off on the right foot. I still had to spend time running around looking for various things. Wooden blocks, iron hooks, bull's-eyes for sheet-leads, were all hard to find; which surprised me since one would expect such traditional gear to be more readily obtainable in the West country than elsewhere. Years before in *Mischief*'s time, I remembered having paid a visit to the Great Grimsby Salt and Fish Co. at Newlyn to buy some composite rope such as was then used by trawlers. I went there again only to find it re-named CoSalt and that CoSalt had gone all "yachty", nothing but plastic and polythene, and fancy clothing for dinghy sailors. The sheet-leads were eventually made for me by a chance-met acquaintance, one-time skipper of the well-known yacht *Tai-Mo-Shan*, who had some lignum vitae on hand. In Cornwall I found a fund of goodwill to be drawn upon, not to me personally but as a man who happened to be fitting out for a serious voyage. So great was the difficulty of finding anchor chain that we looked like being held up for lack of it. Only on the day before sailing John Smith, *Baroque*'s late owner, drove me over to Redruth and we came back with 30 fathoms of $\frac{1}{2}$ in. cable in his station-wagon. Happily the links fitted snugly to the winch gypsy or we should have been sunk.

John Harradine still showed no sign of life until ten days before sailing when I received a telegram from Bergen: "Colorado geophysicist will be a useful addition." It was obviously not in Latin but to me it was equally obscure. I could make nothing of it. Perhaps it was in code or an acrostic but however hard I tried its meaning remained as elusive as the identity of the dark lady of the Sonnets.

The explanation came in a letter a few days later. He had been delayed looking after a sick friend but hoped to join forthwith; meantime he had solved my crew problem by persuading an American scientist, one Steve, to join us. I reacted smartly to this with a telegram to Watford where he had then arrived, telling him on no account to bring Steve. His honour was at stake, came the reply, his promise to take Steve could not be withdrawn. This left me unmoved. My withers, at any rate, were unwrung. Quite apart from Steve's suitability or otherwise we had no spare bunk and a crew of six gave rise to catering and watering problems. John did not turn up until Whit Sunday three days before we were due to sail, bringing with him the unlucky Steve, a lean, gangling chap about 7 ft. long with no sea experience whatsoever. John, as we know, had earmarked the bunk which I had faithfully kept for him. They had brought a mass of gear and Steve, who fancied himself as a carpenter, set about making a shelf over this bunk to accommodate it all. After a day of hammering and sawing up forward I began to wonder what they were doing. The shelf, I found, was to extend over the whole bunk, in effect another bunk on top of the other; possibly it was designed for receiving Steve, either as a stowaway or as a result of presenting me with a *fait accompli*, no longer worth arguing about.

A busy Whit week-end started on the Friday afternoon with the arrival of our stores and their stowage. For the bonded stores the only place left was the "heads" where they were put and duly sealed up by the Customs. Some 60 lbs. of tinned butter for which the ship's chandler had been scouring England were promised for the Tuesday, together with my tobacco which had been over-looked. At home I smoke a pipe with moderation, at sea with duty-free tobacco I smoke like a factory, making hay, so to speak, while the sun shines. Colin Putt with his wife and one of the boys, young Harry, arrived to camp in their Land-Rover in the car-park. We kept young Harry amused over the week-end by sending him afloat in our 7 ft. pram dinghy. *Baroque* had a rubber inflatable, which we never used, and also a life-raft. I viewed this with mixed feelings, since the only voyage on which we had previously carried one had ended in the loss of *Mischief*.

Colin had made a new exhaust pipe which came up through the deck and ended above the coach-roof, whereas the original exhaust had led straight through the ship's side with no "U" bend, thus allowing the sea free access to the engine. The new one made a hellish noise and with the wind in the right quarter the helmsman had the benefit of breathing diesel fumes to remind him of life ashore. He had also made us two massive 15 ft. sweeps out of the old bowsprit. We tried them out later in a Greenland fjord with success, regretting all the more that we had not had them on the previous voyage which might then have ended more happily. Brian Potter came, too, with a fiddle he had made for the table and then busied himself making shelves for our library and for the wireless receiving set. On this we could get weather fore-casts until about 500 miles west and thereafter its main use was for time signals obtained on the Overseas Service of the BBC. We had all the sails up in turn and fitted the leads for the headsail sheets—not perfect but the best that could be done with the dinghy taking up so much of the foredeck. On the Sunday morning, in the middle of what was already considerable confusion, John and Steve arrived to add their quota. Their small car was too small to accommodate 7 ft. of Stephen who had to doss down on the floor by the work-bench. Surveying the busy scene, and mindful of the voyage ahead, I felt like Milton's Satan on the brink of Chaos:

> Pondering his voyage; for no narrow frith
> He had to cross.

That evening Ilan dished up curry for nine, the whole mollified by a bottle of champagne which visiting friends of his had kindly left.

Meantime we had a serious last-minute problem with the engine which threatened delay. When the new stern tube went in it could not be lined up with the engine. The stern tube had to go back for alteration and the engine had to be moved bodily about a ¼ in. We should not know until after the holiday whether this would do the trick and sailing on the 29th May as intended looked unlikely. Colin had to leave on the Tuesday morning, much to my regret, because he could talk to the engineer in his own language, deep calling to deep. Greatly to the discomfort of his passengers he took with him all our spare junk, life-belts, light anchors, the wheel and its worm gear, batteries, and a stainless steel stove-pipe. Perhaps, I was too hasty over the stove-pipe. Just after it had gone I had a telephone call from the makers of the diesel-burning cabin heater that I had ordered three months earlier to say that it was ready. We made do with a Valor paraffin burner. Much the same thing happened with a storm trysail that I had ordered long before. In this case the makers finished it ahead of time and then sat on it, no doubt acting on the Taoist principle that if you practise inaction nothing can be left undone. Coming home across the Atlantic in stormy weather we had frequent occasion to bless them.

To my surprise the stern tube came back on the morning of Wednesday the 30th. The engineer got it in and when the tide had risen enough started the engine to try it out. He was a perfectionist in these matters, talking in terms of thousandths of an inch. Rather grudgingly he thought it might do, to which I, knowing nothing about it, hastily agreed. It was not a difficult conclusion to come to because short of taking it out and starting afresh the engine could not be moved any further.

Accordingly after lunch, on the top of the tide, we left, taking the wise precaution of a tow by the yard launch to see us through the clutter of yachts and yacht moorings outside the harbour. That this had been sensible we soon learnt and re-learnt after several startling episodes in the course of the next four months. The propeller is so far offset that with the engine in gear and the rudder hard over in the contrary direction the boat can barely be kept straight. Turning to port is out of the question. Once clear of the moorings we hoisted sail to a light westerly breeze. By 4 p.m. we were off Pendennis Head and on our own, the two friends who had accompanied us in their boats having turned for home.

CHAPTER ELEVEN

Early Setbacks

We now felt the benefit of starting from so far down Channel. To spend our first night at sea off the Lizard instead of Anvil Point was a welcome change. Even the light wind that prevailed managed to blow out our navigation lamps twice in my watch. No lamps that I have ever had have remained alight with any wind blowing. I have tried colza oil, which is the proper oil to use, and found it made little difference. One wonders how they managed in sailing ships, or in steamers, too, before the days of electricity. Were the lamps better designed or did the lamp boy spend the night relighting them?

A bit more wind when we were south of the Scillies obliged us to reef for the first time and laid out both John and Ilan who succumbed to seasickness. John, looking the picture of misery, spent the night hunched up on the chartroom floor having already discovered the defects of his chosen berth. While lying there he successfully dispelled the pleasure I felt in being at last on our way by saying that he had a septic wisdom tooth and asking to be landed forthwith for treatment. With unusual foresight, on the chance that at the start we might find something seriously wrong with the boat, I had taken the precaution of bringing charts for the south Irish coast and one of Cork harbour. We therefore set a course for Cork and by the Saturday evening were some 35 miles south-east of the Daunt light-vessel. The wind was fresh and fair and in spite of reefing down we would be off the light-vessel by midnight. Early though it was in the voyage some of the drawbacks to a life on the ocean wave had become manifest. The boat was wet and needed a lot of pumping. Besides copious leaks through the topsides there were drips everywhere. The galley skylight leaked badly, the forehatch worse. John's bunk at its foot, with kit lying everywhere and most of it sodden, was a shambles. Ilan carried on cooking but would eat nothing himself except dried apricots. I recalled Peter Marsh, for whose seasickness use and wont had been no remedy, and began to wonder how long Ilan would stick it out. To find a replacement for John, as we might have to do, would be quite enough without having to find another cook as well. For the crew to cook in turn on a long voyage is not satisfactory. Nothing is put back in its right place, no one knows where to find what he wants, and before long both galley and stores are all hugger-mugger.

We hove-to off the Daunt light-vessel at 1 a.m. and waited until after breakfast before going in to anchor in the Quarantine anchorage with our yellow Q flag hoisted. We were in Ireland, moreover it was a Sunday, so one did not expect anything would be done with a rush, but by tea-time, John getting restive, I had begun contemplating a long row ashore to make enquiries. Just then the kindly-disposed skipper of a big yacht out for a Sunday afternoon sail hove-to near by to tell us that if we were waiting for the Customs to come off we might wait for ever. He advised our going to the yacht harbour at Crosshaven where he would show us a mooring and enquire about a dentist for us, and since the entrance was tricky we had better follow him. At the moment we were not ready to move as we were having tea, but I did not mention this as it seemed an unseamanlike reason for delay. By the time we had got our anchor he had gone but we negotiated the entrance on our own and began looking for a vacant mooring. Yachts and yacht moorings stretched for the best part of a mile up river where I decided we would not intrude. Mindful of *Baroque*'s behaviour under power the idea of threading our way past so many expensive yachts looked like madness so we anchored well short of them. Though we were insured against such accidents, collisions are bound to cause delay and possibly some ill-will. The insurance that I had inherited with the boat covered us against all marine risks while cruising in coastal waters. As a matter of interest I had asked the company concerned if they would like to extend the cover to Greenland waters, to which they replied tersely, "On no account."

We spent six days at Crosshaven. John returned from Cork next day with bad news, the dentist having told him that even after treatment he ought to remain within reach for another ten days in case the trouble recurred. In view of this I thought he should quit. With this he agreed, but his suggestion that it was not too late to get hold of his friend Steve fell on deaf ears. Instead I put in the first of several telephone calls to Mylor. During our stay there two young fellows had made enquiries about the voyage and my hopes rested on capturing one or other of them. Knowing the name of neither made things difficult but through the yard manager I got in touch with the first who promised to be with us by the Thursday. So far so good. The Royal Cork Yacht Club, the oldest yacht club of all, had made us welcome and allowed us to use their delightful clubhouse overlooking the river. The crew spent every evening and a good part of the night there.

On the Wednesday evening a telegram advised me that the first man had changed his mind. My second string, I knew, had worked for Bob Pizey and through him we eventually made contact. John Barrett, or Jonno as he called himself, had left Cornwall and gone back to London. He readily agreed to come and hoped to be with us by the Saturday, so provided he remained firm of purpose or was not got at by anxious parents we were back in business. Meantime there were odd jobs to be done on board and shopping expeditions to Cork. The pressure cooker that Ilan got there was money well spent. At Cork the proximity of ships and docks to the shopping centre put me in mind of Reykjavik.

We neglected one job that might have deen done here at the cost of a few days, a job that in the end cost us the best part of a fortnight. The chain plates, which according to the specification of work done in 1970 had been "strengthened and rebolted", were in any case too short, being fastened to only three of the upper planks. Slight cracks showing in the paint on the port side in way of the shrouds indicated that the planks were already under strain. *Mischief* had had the same trouble but only after several voyages did we have to take drastic steps by lengthening the chain plates enough to take up three more planks. There was a boat-yard at Crosshaven where this could have been done—a stitch in time that would have saved several times nine.

After nearly a week of warm, sunny weather that would have been better spent at sea, Saturday, 9th June, came and with it John Barrett. In spite of his youth he had done a good deal of sailing and, as we soon found, seldom hesitated to pass on the benefit of his experience to the rest of us. Garrulity is not, as I thought, confined to the old. Talkers, we are told, are of two kinds, those who talk because they have something to say, and those who talk because they want to say something. Our Jonno was irrepressible either by me or by the crew. One just had to get used to his running commentary as men who work in factories get used to the background of noise. But that is a trifling fault, less irksome most people would say than gloomy reserve, and I was thankful enough for his coming to our aid at short notice, embarking in a strange boat with a strange crew for strange waters. It was a stout effort.

We had already taken on water and fresh bread so at 2 p.m. we got our anchor and motored out. Off the coast that evening we caught a dozen fat mackerel, enough for supper and breakfast. Boiled mackerel are less alluring than when fried or grilled, but Ilan made amends with a fish sauce and topped up with Canary pudding and custard. His sauces were the product of imagination and invention, such as would have deserved or even earned the approval of Dr. Folliott, a reverend gastronome who held that the science of fish sauce was by no means brought to perfection and that a fine field of discovery still lay open in that line. By trolling over the stern one sometimes catches fish, as on this occasion, but more often one merely catches the log-line and produces a devilish tangle. One even catches birds. For some time I had watched a gannet trying to take off from the water close astern. I thought he had a broken wing until at last I realised we had hooked him. We hauled him on board and while Simon, well gloved, held the savagely snapping beak we extracted the hook from his wing.

In spite of the caulking we had done at Crosshaven she still made a lot of water which the Whale pump failed to clear. It worked better when I had dredged out of the well two bucketfuls of coke and oily sludge—a trifle to what Simon got out a month later. By that time the water that was always sloshing about inside had done a real scouring job, like a river in spate. Clearing the well is a dirty job and the best way of cleaning one's hands was to wash-up. Out of gratitude the cook was never allowed to do this chore for which we used hot sea-water and Tepol. The leaks were mainly in the topsides and by 10th June, when we were already 200 miles west of Ireland, the port side chain plates caused us not only alarm but despondency about our making a voyage at all. Besides nearly an inch of daylight to be seen between the planks the adjacent beam and the deck above were lifting. Crossing the Atlantic in that state was not really on, and besides that there would be no chance of effecting repairs in Greenland. Since we must put back to Ireland the obvious place seemed to be Crosshaven where we knew there was a boatyard; the crew, however, reckoned they had seen enough of Crosshaven so we decided to try our luck in Bantry Bay, which was 50 miles nearer and where there should be a yard either at Castletown or at Bantry at the head of bay. The necessity of this decision made it no less hard to take—the loss of 200 miles of westing and an unknown number of days filled me with gloom, besides the possible loss of some of the crew whose confidence in the boat might be on the wane. As to that I need not have worried. They were as determined as her owner to sail *Baroque* to Greenland.

As if sensing the need for haste *Baroque* got a move on, logging over a hundred miles a day for the next two days. By the 16th we were rapidly closing the land in very poor visibility. It was so thick that after supper we hove-to but later that night the weather cleared and the Bull light showed up where expected a few miles to the north-west. There is quite a farmyard hereabouts, the Bull, Cow and Calf rock, and Crow Head. In the morning we made for Castletown gaining the harbour through an excessively narrow entrance. Fortunately, the leading marks were prominently displayed for I had no large-scale chart. After anchoring off the quay Simon and I rowed ashore to consult the Harbour-master. On this Sunday morning the main street was crowded as we stood there talking to Danny O'Neill, brushing off cars, cows and pedestrians, thirsty souls many of the latter making their way from church to the nearest bar in quest, as it were, of more spiritual refreshment. We, too, adjourned to a bar, not so much to drink but so that Danny could use their telephone. He had suggested our going to Lawrence Cove on Bear Island where a friend of his, Finbar Murphy, had a small boatyard. In a back-room Danny talked to Finbar on a telephone that looked like Graham Bell's original model. If it's obsolete it works. Finbar would be going to Cork next morning but he offered to come to Lawrence Cove that evening to see what needed doing. He lived 7 miles from his boatyard at the west end of Bear Island opposite Castletown. The Harbour-master, a friend indeed, offered to pilot us into the cove.

He came off after lunch accompanied by a young man whom I took to be a friend out for the ride but who proved to be the Customs officer, polite, diffident, almost apologising for intruding. The entrance to Lawrence Cove is dog-legged and at high tide an unwary stranger steering a bee-line for the harbour would find himself on a reef. While we were there an English visiting yacht did nearly impale itself before being frightened off by a tumult of shouting. I was glad we had a pilot. We anchored off the quay where one small fishing boat took up all the room available. Finbar's boatyard, which comprised a slipway and a small shed, also had a quay of sorts. If Mylor had seemed the uttermost part of the earth this might have been outer space. I wondered if we had done wisely in coming to a place with one shop, one pub, its only communication with Castletown a ferry run at the whim of the shopkeeper. Meantime, Simon had stripped out all the shelves behind the sink, thus contributing handsomely to Ilan's problems, so that when Finbar came, as he did that evening, he could see what had to be done. Most of the chain plate bolts, we found, were loose, one had sheared, and the wood strongback supporting the plates was far too short. So much for the "strengthening and rebolting" alleged to have been done.

Finbar undertook the job and his quiet, soft-spoken manner inspired confidence. We no doubt mentioned time but he was not a man in a hurry or one who would like being hurried. No man hurries except when catching flies, is the Arab proverb, and since there are few flies at Lawrence Cove there is no reason for anyone to hurry. Only a handful of people live at the place which consists mainly of empty, substantial houses, relics of the days when Bantry Bay was used by the Navy. The old people, Finbar's father for instance, liked to remember the days when the line of battleships anchored in Bear Haven, the roads between the island and the mainland, stretched almost to Castletown—Kipling's "Fleet in Being". Some of the houses have been taken over by a sailing school where young people, many of them French, were taught dinghy sailing. The kedge anchors and their warps which later we had to lay in the small harbour lent an additional hazard to their tuition while they themselves afforded congenial company for my crew when they foregathered every evening at the pub. Mindful of crabbed age and youth I remained hermit-like on board.

The few walks I took about the island were, as Baedeker says, fatiguing and not repaying. It is dotted with small white cottages set amid stony fields with unkempt hedges, where a few cows grazed. Pigs and potatoes, supposedly the Irishman's mainstay, were notably absent, so it must be dairy-farming and not subsistence farming that keeps them alive; fishing too, perhaps, though there were few boats about. We met a marine biologist who had ideas for throwing discarded motor cars into the sea to encourage the lobsters to breed. There were several discarded motor cars to be had, the difficulty seemed to lie with the fishermen. He was a rum chap living there on his own, his sole equipment a wet suit and an aqua-lung, carrying out his research as a private enterprise and finding it hard going. He had a small motor car, one, I thought, that would soon be joining those already discarded, in which he drove me to a fort at the east end of the island. Around it was a beautifully cut dry moat about 20 ft. deep. The fort had a couple of 6 in. guns and though, of course, unoccupied, it was visited periodically by someone from the Irish Army to make sure the guns were still there.

Finbar got back from Cork with the steel for the plates and the necessary bolts on the Wednesday, while Thursday, we learnt, was a public holiday. Meantime Simon had removed the old plates and with two young lads—Finbar's entire work force—was fashioning a massive piece of Iroko wood for a strongback. I had some splicing to do, shortening the wire topping-lifts, and also managed to set up the slack forestay by means of the winch and a length of chain. Ilan went to Castletown with the shopkeeper and brought back some fresh prawns which we had for supper in the form of prawn curry followed by banana sludge, an expressive word, all cooked under difficulties, the galley having been turned upside down and inside out in order to get at the port side. In Ilan we had a cook for all seasons. Local mussels gathered by the crew provided another memorable meal in spite of the time they took to cook.

My hopes that the job could be completed afloat without having to go alongside proved vain, for the new chain plates extended to below the water-line. We tried first alongside Finbar's little quay where we were still afloat and where our marine biologist friend, acting as frogman, failed to get the bolts in. To finish the job we had to go alongside the wharf where she would dry out, so at midnight of 24th June, when the tide served, we put her along-side where she settled down nicely. By next day the job was done. Taking advantage of the wharf we laid out the chain cable in order to repaint the fathom marks (5 fms., 10 fms., 15 fms., etc.) which had already rubbed off. I went to Castletown via the shop-keeper's ferry to cash a cheque and to thank the Harbour-master for his help. He was busy with a Spanish trawler that had been towed in by a compatriot, its net round the propeller. Remembering the German trawler we had seen at Isafjord in similar circumstances I judged this event, distressing enough to the skipper, to be not uncommon. Having settled with Finbar, who had done the best he could for us, we sailed for the third time on 26th June. The loss of twelve days that this caper had cost merely left us more resolved than ever to sail *Baroque* to Greenland.

95

CHAPTER TWELVE

To Greenland

By evening we were well past Mizzen Head, catching another fine lot of mackerel on the way. Even at this early stage the amount of pumping needed to keep the water below the level of the cabin sole provided food for thought. When heeled over with the covering board awash—and the tall mast heeled her over fairly readily—it took 300 strokes a watch to empty the well, which at that time we thought a lot. Reefed down and heeling less she made less water, so the leaks were evidently high up. Later, when rough seas had removed some of the rubbing strake, we found gaps in plank butts that needed caulking. Unfortunately these proved to be not the only source and we just had to get used to living with leaks, as one does. Old salts are said to have welcomed a few generous leaks on the ground that they helped to keep the bilges sweet. If the pumping increased to 1,000 strokes a watch we reefed down and at 2,000 we reckoned it time to heave-to.

We did well the first few days and by 30th June, in spite of having to heave-to more than once, we were nearly 300 miles west of Ireland. 30th June was a Saturday, the day we have our weekly drink. We must have just emptied a gin bottle for Simon took advantage of this to post a letter. He sent no message to mankind, as I suppose he should have done, but merely gave the ship's position, 53° 40′ N, 16° 30′ W., and his address. Some time after we had got home he had a letter to say that the bottle had been found on a beach in Galway Bay east of the Aran Islands, 4 miles south of Black Head, 53° 08′ N. 9° 30′ W., late in August. Using the normal channels, postcards or even first-class mail have been known to take longer. Bottles were emptied and cast into the sea frequently and several of them contained messages but so

13. Umanak Harbour with 3,856 ft. peak.   *Photo: David Meldrum*

14. Huskies watch the harbour activities.   *Photo: David Meldrum*

15. *Baroque* from the
beach at Iglorssuit.
Photo: Ilan Rosengarten

15. *Baroque* from the
beach at Iglorssuit.
Photo: Ilan Rosengarten

16. Sledge at Igdlorssuit.   *Photo: Ilan Rosengarten*

far this is the only one to be found. A more original and far swifter way of posting a letter is recorded in Murphy's monumental work *Oceanic Birds of South America*. On 20th December 1847 a Wandering Albatross was shot off the coast of Chile in 45° 50′ S. 78° 27′ W. and tied to its neck was a vial with a message from a whaling captain: "Dec. 8th 1847. Ship *Euphrates*, Edwards, 16 months out, 2,300 barrels of oil, 150 of it sperm. I have not seen a whale for 4 months. Lat. 43° S. Long. 148° 40′ W. Thick fog, with rain." According to these figures, the albatross had travelled 3,150 nautical miles as the crow flies during the twelve-day interval between the writing of the message and the shooting of the bird.

According to Byron comfort must not be expected by folks that go a pleasuring. I suppose that with increasing age the desire for comfort increases and at the risk of being accused, probably rightly, of having become soft I should say that *Baroque*'s accommodation was sub-standard, at any rate well below that of either *Mischief* or *Seabreeze*. In the saloon there were, as I have said, three berths, the two on the port side, one above the other, occupied by Simon and Brian. The only fault of these two was that they were in the line of fire, or rather water, when a wave hit the cabin skylight on the starboard side. This, of course, was the fault of the skylight, not the bunks, and was remedied by rigging a plastic sheet as a weather dodger. Better still would have been to screw down permanently the skylight as we had done in the galley, but there were occasional fine days when we wanted to open the skylight to introduce some much needed fresh air. The settee berth on the starboard side belonged to Ilan. I had dithered a long time over taking this berth myself because it gave ready access to the chartroom and the cockpit. This settee, however, is the only place in the boat where anyone can sit and its use as a bunk in daytime would preclude this. Besides this, anyone going on deck or coming below, usually in wet oilskins, brushed past it; so I relinquished my claim in favour of the cook who since he had all night in did not need any sleep in the daytime. Ilan rigged a roll-up curtain which he let down at bed-time to fend off passers-by and the odd shower from the skylight; for he, of course, was in the line of fire from that when on the port tack.

Forward of the saloon in the galley was a single bunk on the starboard side, opposite the galley sink, with the foot of the mast between in the middle. Into this single bunk the skipper eventually settled. Perched, perhaps, is *le mot juste*, because it was a good 4 ft. from the floor and one had to climb in and out. Underneath, where there should have been ample stowage space, were three miserable drawers with the habit of falling out. Only by leaning out over the side could one get enough light to read by in daytime, and owing to its proximity to the mast and shrouds all the groans and complaints of the rigging were transmitted to the occupant as if by a sounding board. When on the wind the jib halyards, too, played a most eerie accompaniment, like the mournful howl of a pack of wolves baying the moon only more intimidating. Compensations were the gratifying smells of cookery and the appreciable rise in temperature when the Primus stoves were going. Moreover, in this bunk no shower baths need be expected, only a persistent drip from the deck beams. Plastic guttering fixed to the beams with drawing pins were the answer to this. Indeed, we all rigged ingenious aqueducts of which Archimedes himself would not have been ashamed.

The bunk forward of the galley on the port side opposite the work bench probably had the highest rainfall, as it were. John Harradine had unwisely chosen this and John Barrett inherited it. The fore hatch just above was the most generous source of water, but there were others. John or Jonno lived under a more or less permanent polythene tent. Besides high humidity he had the benefit of being thrown about more being so far forward; but John, like Shakespeare's "wet sea-boy upon the giddy mast", had an infinite capacity for sleep, spent more time on his back than anyone, even foregoing meals in favour of sleep, and made no complaints. The mention of meals reminds me of another slight imperfection in our arrangements. The table I had put in on top of the water tank, for which Brian had made a patent adjustable fiddle, came to be used merely as somewhere to put things. No one sat round and ate off it in civilised fashion. Three of us sat on the settee out of reach of the table with our plates in our laps, the fourth in a corner on the opposite side also out of reach of the table. But sailors can hardly expect to eat off tables. On a five months' voyage in 1964 to Heard Island in a 50-ton schooner ten of us ate our meals in a cabin rather smaller than *Baroque*'s, occupied, too, by a large gas stove on which the meals were cooked. There may have been a small table but at meal-times some of the ten sat on it while the rest perched or stood where they could clutching their plates.

Dr. Johnson had great contempt for anyone so lacking in ideas, so feeble-minded, such a blockhead in fact, that he needs must fall back on the weather as a topic of conversation. The great Cham of literature himself would have found it hard to describe a voyage without mentioning the weather. Some long-distance voyagers mention nothing else and even those who are more restrained— the weather being what it often is—cannot help appearing querulous. This is not really so. Most amateur sailors who go to sea for pleasure want that pleasure to be occasionally spiced with the stresses and strains that usually accompany bad weather, spiced even with some hazards and the bright eye of danger. That this is what appeals to men, though on a more lofty plane, is what Garibaldi knew when he offered "neither pay, nor quarters, nor provisions; but hunger, thirst, forced marches, battles, and death". On those carefree, sunny days, the wind free, the sails full, the crew will no doubt express their delight. "This is what we came for" will be the cry, but if of the right sort their happiness, though unexpressed, will be the same when wet and cold, struggling against adverse conditions.

June and July are reckoned as quiet months in the North Atlantic. Quiet is a relative term and much depends on the kind of vessel concerned, a ship of 30,000 tons, say, or a boat of 30 tons. Quiet or not the weather at least offered variety, from flat calms to gales, fog, drizzle, torrential rain, even some occasional sunshine. We had no trouble in making northing, reaching within a hundred miles of the latitude of C. Farewell (59° 46′ N.) when we were still 300 miles to the east. To be a hundred miles south of the cape is not an excessive margin because on account of the possible presence of icebergs vessels are advised to give it a berth of at least 70 miles.

When far from land it is not of vital importance to know exactly where one is, yet without at least one daily fix the mariner tends to feel frustrated. Even in summer in the North Atlantic sights are not all that readily obtainable owing either to heavy and persistent overcast, rain, fog or high seas. Apart from the roughness caused by a gale the wind may blow so hard that watering eyes make it impossible to take sights. I see from the log that for four successive days south of C. Farewell we were without any noon sight, the sight that provides an accurate latitude, without which the other sights when worked out may indicate a position that is in fact many miles out. Star sights are particularly hard to obtain. It is more often cloudy at dawn and dusk than at midday. If the sky clears it will be at night when, even if it is bright moonlight, the prudent navigator will put little faith in any star sights he may take, and, of course, north of, say, Lat. 58°, in summer it is not dark enough for stars to be visible. In these circumstances the peevish navigator feels inclined to agree with the remarks attributed to Lord Jeffery: "Dam the solar system; bad light, planets too distant, pestered with comets, feeble contrivance; could make a better with ease."

We met only one ship on this passage. On 12th July in Lat. 57° N. the wind taking off after a night at nearly gale force, the *Haralde*, registered in Monrovia, startled us by coming within about twenty yards down wind and passing very slowly across our bows. In my panic-stricken eyes he appeared much closer. I really feared our bowsprit would hit her or rather that he was about to break our bowsprit. A chap on the bridge with no loud-hailer shouted unintelligibly into the wind, and not content with that they turned and came back almost as close on the other side. I expect they wanted to know if we were all right, which was friendly of them but frightening. A gam with another ship in mid-ocean is a great event but for such social occasions the weather needs to be good.

After his too prolonged bout of malaise Ilan had long since found his feet; our fears that he might prove to be another Peter Marsh were finally set at rest. A long voyage can be made or marred by the cook and the meals he provides. At sea meals predominate even more than they do on land and in the inevitable monotony of a long passage the crew are apt to become like Carlyle's gluttonous Jutes and Angles, "men who see the sun rise with no other hope but that they shall fill their bellies before it sets". For breakfast porridge was the general rule, providing for most of the crew a convenient way of conveying to their mouths large quantities of sugar; though Ilan became a dab hand at turning out omelettes from dried egg of which we had a large amount. These would be generously laced with Tabasco or with melted cheese, or sometimes filled with curry left over from supper. Curry for breakfast used to be the normal thing on ships plying

to the East or on any ships that had Goanese or Lascar cooks and
stewards. On *Mischief*'s last voyage south, however, left-over
curry for breakfast had disgusted one of the crew and the high
words that followed this refusal to eat what was given had led
ultimately to his deserting at Montevideo and taking most of the
crew with him. The traveller, as the proverb says, should have
the back of an ass to bear all and the mouth of a hog to eat what
is set before him.

For lunch we rang the changes on sardines, pilchards, spam, or
cheese, with either coffee or cocoa. Peanut butter and Marmite
were popular, while hard white cabbage and raw onions provided
a salad of sorts. Tea at 4.30 p.m. was not to be lightly missed, for
besides bread, butter, and jam Ilan frequently baked us a cake
or a sort of shortbread made from Quaker Oats. Bread is no great
problem on a Greenland voyage. Bread taken at the start will last
nearly ten days before going mouldy and after that we go on to
twice-baked, sliced bread re-baked, which if properly done and
kept in a plastic sack lasts indefinitely. It takes up too much space
to carry enough for the whole voyage but on arriving in Greenland
one has rye-bread (*rugbrod*) which again lasts for months. This
stuff also has the advantage that the crew find it less palatable
and eat less of it as time goes on. Our twice-baked bread gave
out two days before reaching Greenland and Ilan bridged the gap
with chapatties and soda-bread. Proper bread could be baked at
sea even on a Primus stove, but in the absence of a hot sun or a
warm place in the boat the difficulty is to get the dough to rise.
Moreover, freshly baked bread is far too palatable and to satisfy
the crew the cook would be at it all day and every day, using far
too much paraffin.

For supper, the highlight of the day, Ilan exerted his powers
and the rougher it was the more he liked to defy the elements by
dishing up something elaborate. His sauces have already received
honourable mention. Of some one might say, like the French
gastronome, "*Avec cette sauce on mangerait son père.*" Curries, of
course, *pasta sciuta, rissotto,* lentil soup (a meal in itself), stew
with dumplings, fried rice, sausage and mash, potato pie with
grated cheese on top (the cheese toasted with a blow-lamp), and
one or two Greek dishes, *moussala* for one if I have the name right.
Besides the duffs that took pride of place as a second course, open
tarts of short pastry filled with dried fruit figured largely. The

duffs were all what might be called visions of the higher gluttony, chocolate duffs with chocolate sauce, feathery Canary puddings, or weightier belly-timber like spotted dog, rich in raisins and sultanas. No grounds for mutiny on that score:

> We hadn't been but a week at sea
> When the duff, it don't seem to please,
> It hadn't the riches of raisins and sichness
> So we ups and we mutinies.

All this cookery had to be done on a double-burner gimballed stove and a single-burner with no gimbals. Space had not allowed of gimbals for the latter and happily my fears that on this account it would not be much use at sea proved groundless. The galley being amidships, and Pilot cutters sea-kindly boats, Ilan had no trouble with it even in rough weather. Except on the way home when during a gale it jumped off its stand and sustained a hair-crack which put it out of action.

This domestic digression has led me away from the weather. A gale that lasted longer than we liked set us nearly 60 miles to the south and two almost windless days went by before we got the southerly wind we needed to get round C. Farewell. The warm southerly wind brought with it rain and fog that prevailed for the next three dank and dismal days. On the morning of 19th July the weather brightened and we made a far from precise landfall somewhere to the west of the cape. The southernmost point of Greenland does not stand out boldly and unmistakably like some more famous sea-marks, the Cape itself for instance, or C. Horn. Like them, however, or any cape at the extremity of a land-mass it can at times breed dirty weather. As the *Arctic Pilot* remarks: "C. Farewell is notorious for foul weather and heavy seas."

Soon after sighting the land we were overtaken by a violent thunder-storm accompanied by lightning, wind and rain. At the height of this short-lived storm we ran fast past two icebergs, the first we had met. When the sun came out that evening I got a sight confirming our position, or at least confirming that we were at last west of the cape. By then we had twenty-five bergs in sight. Since we were not more than 15 miles from the coast I had expected to see pack-ice as well, and the fall in the sea temperature from 5·75°C. to 0·25°C. indicated that it could not be far away. As usual on these voyages in waters seldom covered by British ships we were keeping a meteorological log for the Meteorological Office; though unlike the other three hundred-odd voluntary observing ships that keep meteorological logs we cannot transmit observations at the time they are made. I regret the sudden transition from Fahrenheit to Centigrade or Celsius. It is really the fault of the Meteorological Office who, having gone all metric, supplied us for this voyage with thermometers marked in the latter scale.

The fog that prevailed after supper warned us that later in the night, during the darker hours either side of midnight, we would be well advised to heave-to. If the fog is not utterly dense icebergs can generally be seen in time for a slow-moving ship to avoid them. Not always, or at least not without disquiet. At 11 p.m. Brian in a state of agitation rushed down, muttered something about going about, and rushed back on deck. Not waiting to put any more clothes on I was on deck in a minute in time to see that we should just clear a large berg some thirty yards to port. At a safe distance from it we hove-to. Next morning I put on my winter woollies, had the Valor paraffin stove lit, and ordered the chart-room door to be kept shut. The stove did raise the cabin temperature a little and was always good for drying clothes.

Davis Strait may not be as bad as the Strait of Belle Ile, the place where they invented fog, but it enjoys quite a lot, sometimes merely in shifting banks, at other times a wide-spreading blanket. Navigation became uncertain. Steering east of north on a course that would close the land, the wind fresh and visibility under a thousand yards, I had an uneasy night. Early on the 22nd there was still nothing to be seen until at last around 9 a.m. we sighted a high island a few hundred yards away. Later the fog cleared sufficiently for us to identify this island, 700 ft. high and a half-mile long, as Qioqe, some 30 miles south of Frederikshaab. That we could close the land like this without encountering any ice showed a great change from the conditions we had met in 1970. The fact that we were now a fortnight later makes some difference, but in that year no ships could enter Frederikshaab and we ourselves were fast in the pack some 10 miles north of it. This, by the way, is not ice that has remained over from winter. It is what the Danes call the Storis, or Great Ice, consisting of old and massive floes from the Polar Sea brought all the way down the east coast of Greenland by the current, round C. Farewell, and up the west coast as far as or beyond Frederikshaab where it begins to disperse and disintegrate.

Closing the land again on the 25th we sighted what I took to be the Hellfiske Øer, a straggling group of islets and rocks marked at their southern extremity by a beacon which we failed to see. Like the east coast, the west coast of Greenland is strewn with islands and islets, barren rocks all very much alike. Unless one can spot the rare one crowned by a beacon identification is largely guesswork. We guessed right this time. Having stood out for some 6 miles we went in again expecting to see and identify Faeringehavn, as we did that evening in the fading light. Lighthouses are still rarities on the Greenland coast and they are not the structures we are accustomed to seeing. We had gone into Faeringehavn in 1970 after being released by the ice and I do not remember any lights. The latest edition of the *Pilot* now told us that "a light is exhibited at an elevation of 53 ft. from a concrete column *3 ft. high* situated on the summit of Den Smukke Ø", and sure enough there it was blinking every five seconds. On a filthy night of wind and rain we stood out once more to heave-to at midnight.

Godthaab lay only about 20 miles to the north and all we had to do was to find the entrance to the fjord, a task that looked fairly hopeless in the fog that enveloped us next morning. As we motored and sailed north the visibility slowly improved and at midday we sighted numerous islands. Several of the islands off the fjord entrance carry beacons, none of these showed any. When the sun broke through briefly I got a snap sight close to the meridian which put us 5 miles north of the entrance, so we started south and presently made out the essential island with its beacon. Although the fjord entrance is wide the navigable channel is restricted to a cable's width between the beaconed island and a reef.

The fjord is long as well as wide. Godthaab itself, the capital of West Greenland, is 15 miles up, while the main fjord and its branches extend as far as the inland ice 70 miles from the coast. Around the inner fjord was the so-called West Settlement of the Norse colonists comprising some ninety farms of which seventy have been located. The Eastern Settlement, or Osterbydd, founded by Eric the Red in A.D. 986 around Julianehaab in southwest Greenland was much larger, comprising three hundred or more farms. It had its church and a bishop. When all communication with Europe ceased in the fourteenth century, probably because of worsening ice conditions, the colonists died out. Besides the ruins of Viking homesteads dotted about, moving testimonies to perhaps the hardiest colonists of all time, the region is mountainous, so that Godthaab, which on four occasions hitherto I have regarded merely as a place of refreshment before pushing on elsewhere, would amply repay a long visit. As we were already too late, I thought, for Ellesemere Island we might have stayed there this time had I not more or less promised to meet a friend further north. Nor would the crew have been happy had we stopped short of the Arctic Circle.

CHAPTER THIRTEEN

North to Igdlorssuit

We secured that evening alongside a fishing vessel close under the rock wall that bounds the west side of the harbour. On this wall are painted the names of numerous visiting ships, among them the only two British names, H.M.S. *Whitby* and *Mischief*. I had half forgotten our having painted it and the familiar name moved me almost to tears. We had left this record in 1963 and before we left this time we repainted it. In Wales the more fervent Nationalists sometimes express their feelings on suitable rock faces and are duly condemned for vandalism by all right-minded people, but in this case, where I was personally involved, I felt proud as well as sad. We ought to have found the time and a space on the wall on which to paint *Baroque*.

Greenland is not immune from the fashionable disease of "growth". The harbour had changed almost out of recognition. Along the foot of the rock wall where formerly two or three vessels might be anchored, was now a long wooden jetty with fishing vessels moored three abreast. The main quay has been lengthened and large warehouses built on it, and room has been made for a fish quay and an adjacent fish factory.

Nevertheless, the same informality prevails and for a visiting yacht at any rate, entry to a port could hardly be simpler—no papers, no passports, no Customs, no harbour dues. I was about to add that such a happy state of affairs in this form-filling age must be unique until I remembered Cork where officialdom had ignored us, and Castletown where the Customs officer had almost apologised for coming on board.

According to the *Pilot* the population of Godthaab is now about 6,000, of whom 5,000 are Eskimos, or Greenlanders as they are now called. In 1960 it was about 3,000. The *Pilot*, by the way, which as regards navigation one assumes to be infallible, credits Godthaab with a narrow-gauge railway connecting the harbour with the town, whereas there is no such thing. The town was founded as long ago as 1721 by Hans Egede, the Lutheran missionary, although the great Elizabethan seaman-explorer John Davis is believed to have anchored in Godthaab fjord on his first voyage in search of the North-west Passage in 1585. He named it Gilbert's Sound, presumably in honour of Sir Humphrey Gilbert. On our visits in the early sixties Godthaab had impressed me as a raw, thriving pioneer town with much work to be done and no time to be lost, and that impression did not need much revision in 1973. The town itself, a mile from the harbour, is scattered over a peninsula of solid rock interspersed with boggy hollows where cotton grass used to flourish. On this unpromising site all foundations have to be blasted out, telephones and power lines carried overhead on a forest of poles, the drains on the surface, and the water supplied in boxed conduits to prevent it freezing in winter. Hans Egede's house built of local stone has been preserved, but all other buildings are of imported materials. The private houses painted in lively colours—green, red, yellow, blue —are now almost lost among sober-hued blocks of three-storey flats.

Either in supermarkets or shops one can buy pretty well anything one is likely to need at not much more than European prices. Only in the matter of copper-sheet did we have any bother. Having tried all the likely and unlikely places a helpful taxi-driver took us to a huge Government depot covering acres of ground which seemed to stock everything needed for building a town from scratch. Several lower grade officials were nonplussed and it was not until we reached the man with whom the buck had to stop that we got what we wanted. When confronted with enough sheeting to copper-bottom a battleship I felt a bit of a fool asking for two square feet. However, they cut it off and after a lot of paper-work—we might have been signing a treaty—we got our copper. A Seaman's Home down by the harbour was new and most welcome to us as a place where we could get shower-baths and meals. Even at Godthaab one cannot escape television. On our first night at the Seaman's Home we watched Frank Sinatra in colour. Besides the two hotels which we assumed would be beyond our means there are two low-grade cafeterias. We had some food at one around midday but by night apparently one could only drink. Putting my head inside one night I found it crammed with Greenlanders in convivial mood and hastily withdrew. The old Kristinemut where formerly we had gone for beer and whale steak had become a hotel.

Throughout our short stay the weather remained cool and wet. Patches of snow still lay about at sea level and we were told that three weeks earlier there had been a heavy fall. It is not always thus. On previous visits we had suffered from heat and mosquitoes and the Danish workmen by the roadside, sweating as they wielded a pneumatic drill, all wore face veils. Expecting to use a lot of fuel on the way north we wanted a 25-gallon drum of oil. Rather than imperil others as well as ourselves by moving *Baroque* alongside in the congested harbour we went to a pump at the old harbour across the peninsula and brought back the drum in a taxi. The springs just held out. Having rolled the drum into the water at the head of the harbour we left it for John to tow off with the dinghy. Oil drums are not all that towable but a friendly motor launch came to his assistance.

The night before we were due to sail the wind began blowing from north-west with some ferocity. By dawn the bow lines of the fishing vessel to which we were secured had parted with the result that our counter began to take some hard knocks from a vessel lying astern. Starting the engine, we let go our warps, dropped the big Fisherman anchor under-foot, and veered cable until we were riding clear. All that morning it blew hard. Brian, who is not an expert waterman, tried to put Ilan ashore, a matter of twenty yards or so. The wind took charge and off went the pram dinghy down the harbour with every prospect of being bashed against the rocks at the far end. The harbour launch, seeing their plight, steamed after them, picked them up, and landed them. When Brian started back with the dinghy he once more lost his battle with the wind and once more the harbour launch went to the rescue. This time, taking no chances, they came alongside and handed over first Brian and then the dinghy.

When the wind dropped that afternoon we went over to the main quay for water. The nearest we could get was outside two other vessels across which they passed us a long hose. Having collected Ilan and the stores he had bought we were ready to go. Twenty loaves of black bread, each loaf nearly 2 ft. long, took some carrying, as well as sacks of potatoes and onions. Never board a ship without an onion, is sound doctrine.

The Harbour-master, hearing we were bound for Umanak fjord, gave me a letter for my friend Dr. Drever whom he knew, and at 6 p.m. we cast off. On a windless evening we had a long, noisy chug down the fjord. Further north in Davis Strait in summer the winds are generally light and most often northerly. We were three weeks late and I reckoned it would be nearly the end of August before we reached Ellesmere Island, just in time to start the voyage home. Instead we would make for Igdlorssuit, a small settlement in Lat. 71° N. where we had been on the first Greenland voyage in 1961. Mountains are plentiful in that region and Dr. Drever would be there until 13th August. It is only some 450 miles from Godthaab, but we were to need all the time allowed.

Off this coast, from Frederikshaab in the south up to Lat. 70° N., there are fishing banks rich in cod and halibut. It surprised me that we met hardly any trawlers and we were particularly disappointed not to see any of the famous Portuguese three-masted schooners, a common enough sight in the sixties. These schooners, after fishing on the Grand Banks in early summer, proceeded to the Greenland banks to complete their catch of cod, all by hand-lining from dories. Having anchored on the bank the schooners launched their dories of which each carried some sixty. These are flat-bottomed, about 14 ft. long, without thwarts, centre board, buoyancy tanks, or rudder, the absence of such fittings making for easy stowage in nests on the schooner's deck. For sailing out and back to the parent ship a mast is stepped and jib and lugsail set. The doryman has a 3,000 ft. long line with some 500 hooks on "snoods", which he baits with frozen squid, sardines or caplin. Tossing up and down in a dinghy, handling the line with half-frozen hands, the baiting of 500 hooks, and worse still removing the hook from the mouths of cold, slimy, flapping cod, is a job that only men bred to the life would undertake. Having filled his dory with cod until only a few inches of freeboard remain, the doryman sails back to the parent ship, and standing up in his heaving dory gaffs the catch one by one on to the schooner's deck.

If there were any trawlers or Portuguese schooners about we met none, instead we were pestered by drifters engaged in netting salmon. Particularly on the Little and Great Hellefiske banks north of Godthaab and beyond Holsteinborg we kept sighting the dan buoys marking the nets and their attendant boats— Norwegian, Spanish or Greenlanders—standing by. Though not as lethal as icebergs these nets seemed to me to constitute a worse menace for the unwary in that part of Davis Strait. Twice we fell foul of nets, on both occasions with the skipper at the helm. This was, perhaps, just as well. It gave rise to no harsh words, as otherwise it might have done, and it gave the crew a laugh and a feeling, if only temporary, of superior skill—what a fool the man must be to run into a marked net, not once but twice. The nets are about a mile long, with small plastic floats on top and at each end a dan buoy, a buoy with a 6 ft. pole and flag. Having laid its net the boat stands by two or three miles off until it is time to haul. This distance between the net and the boat that layed it, as if trying to disclaim responsibility, caused us some inconvenience. I never understood why they lay off so far unless they thought the boat's presence might scare away the salmon.

Three days out from Godthaab, on the evening of 2nd August, having closed the land we had gone about and were standing out to sea. On this placid evening, admiring the sunlit coast astern, I may not have been fully alert, nor as yet had we fully hoisted in the implications of dan buoys with stationary boats in the offing. When a line of yellow plastic floats suddenly appeared ahead almost under our bows I thought we might safely slide over them. I think we might, too, had it not been for the broken keel band which we had not been able to put right at Mylor. Firmly held by the net, as we promptly were, we handed the sails and did all we could to free ourselves by hauling on the net from various directions. No go. The small Greenlander boat to whom the net belonged lay about two miles away and took no notice. The first rocket we fired, a parachute flare, failed to flare so we touched off an orange smoke canister. *Baroque*'s equipment which I had inherited had been sparse enough except in the way of distress signals and fireworks of various kinds—no doubt previous owners had felt they might be needed. Roused by our orange smoke screen the Greenlanders soon came to our assistance. Having launched their dinghy they passed us a rope and while the men in the dinghy held on to the net they towed us off stern first. We came off easily enough, no damage to the net, and no hard feelings on either side.

The very next day, though this time with some excuse, I committed a similar blunder, a blunder which caused far more delay and which had consequences for both parties. Having tacked twice during the night, for the wind was northerly, we were again standing out to sea when I marked down a dan buoy ahead and its fellow half a mile away. Steering carefully to round the buoy to leeward I noticed too late a small red dan buoy some fifty yards further out to which the net, rather unfairly, extended. We were properly caught, and before long made matters worse by drifting on to another net. We hauled away on the net and this time with some success, for we extracted a fine, big salmon and consigned it forthwith to the galley. A few other fish in sight in the net were unfortunately out of reach. There were several boats hanging about in the offing, none of which paid the least attention. A yacht sailing in those waters would surely attract some attention and if it suddenly lowered its sails and remained stationary by a dan buoy one would have expected the penny to drop.

A smoke canister had worked with the Greenlanders so we tried another. If anyone in those boats 2 miles away thought we were on fire they remained admirably calm. Then we got out our parachute flares and soon had the technique worked out. Sticks had to be fashioned for the rocket and the vertical exhaust-pipe by the doghouse made a fine launching pad. Each of us in turn had the privilege of touching off a rocket, with some jealous competition as to whose would fly highest and burn longest. Nearly two hours elapsed and five rockets had been fired before one of the distant boats started steaming towards us. One felt that had we been sinking or on fire it would have been a close run thing. The Norwegian who arrived got his net free fairly easily and told us that the net we were really wrapped up in belonged to his mate who had gone back to Holsteinborg but whom he would call up by radio telephone. Both boats came from Alesund. While waiting we watched the first boat haul his net. It came in over a roller with a man standing by extracting the fish. I reckoned that for every two yards of net they had a salmon, so that a half-mile of net catches a lot of fish. In view of the number of boats at work that came within our limited vision it is not surprising that our salmon rivers are feeling the effect.

When the other boat at last arrived they passed us a line and tried towing from various angles without success. Finally, with their consent if not approval, we began hacking away at the nylon net and its numerous ropes. We could not reach far down and when at length free we still had a long streamer of net and rope attached to the keelband. Some of this was round the propeller and the rest we lashed to the bulwarks to keep out of harm's way. Under way again and steering north we then found that the first Norwegian boat was busy re-laying his net right across our course. True he was flashing a lamp to warn us but in my aggrieved eyes he seemed to be acting with malice aforethought. We went about just in time to avoid a third incident. The salmon steaks that we ate that night more than made up for the loss of a few hours and five parachute flares. I thought the crew might have proposed a vote of thanks.

In the early part of the voyage I may have overpainted the charms of Greenland, laying some stress on the weather we should enjoy, cloudless skies, twenty-four hours of unbroken sunshine, the calm blue water dotted with picturesque icebergs glinting in the sun; whereas up to Godthaab the reality had been roughish seas, rain, a minimum of sun, and fog in which the vague shape of icebergs loomed menacingly. As we had found years before, one must go north, north at least of the Arctic Circle, to enjoy halcyon weather. This magic circle (Lat. 66° 30') was not crossed until 5th August, until when we had been beating against fresh northerly winds and not doing very well. Igdlorssuit by 13th August, unaided by the engine, was by no means in the bag. To celebrate crossing the Arctic Circle we ate and drank rather more than usual. It offered an excuse for an additional drink beyond that of the customary Saturday night tot, we opened a Christmas pudding, while John produced a magnum of Spanish wine bought in Godthaab for this occasion. No certificates were issued to the crew, as I believe is done for the passengers on cruise ships, nor were all hands piped to bathe and skylark.

On the 6th, taking advantage of the first calm, windless day, we began clearing the propeller, and by patiently poking and probing with a boathook John at last succeeded. Our chances of reaching Igdlorssuit in time were thus improved. But clearing the net from the keelband defied all our efforts. We tried with a knife lashed to a boathook, and we tried attaching a 56 lb. weight, a piece of ballast, to give a vertical downwards pull. John, with no wet suit or any under-water gear, even offered to jump in. With

17. Abraham Zub, grand old man of Igdlors-suit. Formerly a great hunter, with a medal from King Frederick of Denmark. He is demonstrating a string figure (cat's cradle), a favourite Greenlander ploy.

Photo: H. I. Drever

18. Motor boat with kayak belonging to the village headman, Otto Ottosen, seen in the bows.   *Photo: H. I. Drever*

19. Glacier on Upernivik.   *Photo: Ilan Rosengarten*

the sea temperature at 3°C. I discouraged this, although, as I reflected, it might have silenced him for a bit if not for ever. While all this was going on we were drifting vaguely in fog towards the Qagsit Islands, two islands 10 miles out from the coast extensively surrounded by foul ground. In fact we were further inshore than we imagined.

Fog plays some queer tricks. At 2 a.m., Brian who had just relieved me drew my attention to a dark object apparently not more than a couple of hundred yards away. Staring at it for a long time through binoculars neither of us could decide whether it was a rock, a great bunch of kelp, or some sea monster. Brian suggested rowing across to see, a matter of minutes. When the fog had thinned a little we recognised it as an island a good 2 miles away, certainly a long row. Later that morning, still in fog, only the lucky glimpsing of two islands to the west showed that we were inside the Qagsit. We took steps accordingly and went out to sea.

Another flat calm on 7th August allowed us to have another go at ridding the boat of its incubus the net, when we merely succeeded in breaking a boathook. By now it had become a race against time. By the 10th we had got up to Lat. 68° N. leaving five days to reach Lat. 71°, or rather more than 200 miles since we had to go round north of Disko Island. With time in hand I would have taken the longer way inside Disko through the strait called Vaigat where there is the largest concentration of freshly calved icebergs anywhere. Icebergs of all shapes and sizes, some like fortresses with sheer sides, others with pinnacled towers like glistening cathedrals, all floating serenely on the stillest of blue seas. As the *Pilot* records:

> in June, after the break-up of the winter ice, thousands of icebergs some from 200 ft. to 300 ft. high, drift backwards and forwards with the tidal streams, or in other directions according to the wind; these bergs render navigation dangerous and anchorage impossible.

Later on, as in August, when many of the bergs have gone out to sea, the Vaigat is not as bad as it is painted. When returning through it in August 1961 we managed well enough. These bergs are calved from the numerous glaciers that descend into the Vaigat from the ice-cap, two very large glaciers near Jakobshavn being principal offenders. For a visit to Jakobshavn one might

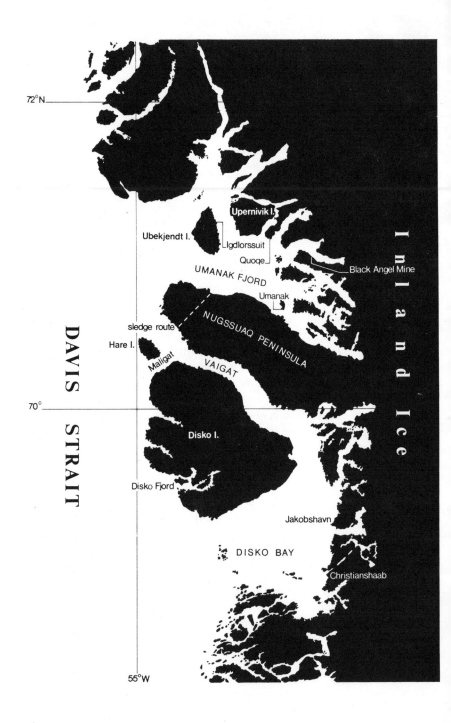

need a more compelling reason than curiosity. As the *Pilot* says:

> A peculiarity of Jakobshavn is the so-called *kanel* produced by the calving of large icebergs or by a discharge of ice from Jakobshavn Isfjord. Without warning a large or small wave comes rolling into the inner harbour; the water is violently disturbed and covered with white foam, while seaweed and vegetation on the bottom are torn up by the roots. The *kanel* appears in September and may be violent enough to tear vessels from their moorings.

Having seen the glaciers where they originate, with bergs a daily sight and, when becalmed, recognising old friends, marking their progress or lack of progress, seeing and hearing one split, or even capsize, one naturally becomes interested in their ultimate fate. Nearly all Arctic bergs originate from the glaciers of east and west Greenland and it is reckoned that 70 per cent come from the regions of Disko and of Umanak to the north. The twelve biggest glaciers of this area are estimated to discharge 5,400 bergs annually. The flow of the current carries the bergs northwards up the Greenland coast, round the head of Baffin Bay, and then southward down the Labrador coast to the region of Newfoundland. The time taken by a berg to reach Newfoundland, and, of course, only a few of the bigger ones survive that long, varies greatly. Shape, strandings, variations in local current, and other factors, all play a part. It is possible for two bergs calved from the same glacier on the same day to be separated by one or even two years in the time of their arrival at the Tail of the Grand Bank.

Slowly we worked our way up the west coast of Disko Island, frequently in fog, and using the engine more and more as time began to run out. On the 11th we ran it all night, thus ensuring for some of us a sleepless night. For the amateur, navigation is never an exact science and if fog has added to his uncertainties he must be prepared for some unexpected sights. North of Disko Island is Hare Island and between them is a 5-mile-wide channel called Maligat. Thinking that the channel might be infested with bergs I had decided to go north of Hare Island and on the 12th, until the fog lifted a little, that is what I thought we were doing. Land then showed up on either side and that to the north might or might not be Hare Island. There was another puzzle. What looked like another island lay to the north-east, whereas if we were in the

Maligat strait looking to the east we should have seen an unbroken line of coast on the far side of the Vaigat. According to the chart the only place that might conceivably agree with what we saw was Disko fjord, 30 miles to the south, and that was too discouraging to believe. He who knows not where to go is in no hurry to move. Further prolonged study of chart and *Pilot* revealed that across the land to the east that we were looking at, the Nugssuaq peninsula, ran a wide valley, a well-known Greenlander sledging route. I guessed then that what looked like an island to the northeast was actually the tip of the peninsula and that fog lying in the wide valley had given it the appearance of an island. On that assumption we pressed on and although fog still hung over the valley we soon satisfied ourselves that we were at the northern end of the Vaigat and not in Disko fjord. Having rounded the tip of Nugssuaq peninsula our next mark was Ubekendt Island, 20 miles away, with Igdlorssuit another 15 miles up its eastern side. We had to motor all that night and a good part of the following day, hoisting our sails as we approached the settlement, not on account of any wind, but by way of a gesture and to astonish the natives. There is no harbour, hardly even a bay, and as we anchored off the beach of black sand at 3 p.m. on the 13th we were boarded by another and quite unexpected friend. This was Frank George of the Royal Institute of Navigation and for the life of me I could not think what had brought him to Igdlorssuit. In the role of surveyor he had come to measure glacier movement on the neighbouring island of Upernivik, not that glacier movement has any bearing on navigation, even in Greenland waters. I lost no time in going ashore to be greeted by the man I had expected to see, my friend Dr. Drever, wearing a deerstalker hat and in spite of that looking every inch a benign and comparatively learned professor.

CHAPTER FOURTEEN

To the Mountains

In recent years St. Andrews University, with which I have a loose, unacademic connection, have built a hut at Igdlorssuit, as has, more recently, Manchester University. The two are side by side well clear of the settlement. In the matter of the hut Dr. Drever, who has made several visits and who for many years has made a study of the rocks of Ubekendt Island, was the moving spirit. The layman who thinks that a few hours or even days devoted to the studying of a piece of rock would be more than enough is seriously mistaken. Geologists, as even the layman should know, have their own vast time-scale, and work accordingly. I believe that some of the Ubekendt rock is similar to that which has been brought back from the moon, but, as Tallulah Bankhead would say, there may be less in this than meets the eye. In the course of his visits Dr. Drever has conceived a great liking and respect for the people of the settlement with whom he has had close relations, and is rightly concerned for the future of this self-contained, self-sufficient happy community. In fact his interest in them now threatens to outdo his interest in igneous rocks. On this occasion, largely through him, what was called the Scottish West Greenland Project had been active on the island since July, its main objective, besides several others, being "the reconnaissance of possible sites on Ubekendt for a field centre designed to promote cross-cultural communication between people with an Eskimo cultural inheritance and people with other cultures". Besides Dr. Drever, the party included two high-powered professors (an American and a Dane) of Eskimology and Sociology. On a slightly more frivolous plane one cross-cultural feature, introduced some years ago by Dr. Drever, had been a sort of local Derby Day, a day of jollification, the big event a race for kayaks from Umanak to Igdlorssuit, a distance of 50 miles. We missed this by arriving too late. I was told that entries for this formidable endurance test are falling off. Possibly the Greenlanders are becoming soft, like ourselves, or are learning from us that sporting events deserve more tangible rewards than honour and glory.

The settlement seemed to me to be much the same as when we had last seen it in 1961. Very little "growth" here one was thankful to note. Like all other Greenlanders the people of Igdlorssuit are far from being of pure Eskimo descent, of whom nowadays there are few if any left. In the course of the last two centuries seamen and whalers of various nationalities and Danish officials and traders have seen to that. Yet they and their way of life appeared to us to have some resemblance to the real thing; the huskies, of which each family has a sledge team or more, the sledges lying about, the kayaks stored high up out of the reach of dogs, the racks of shark meat and cod drying in the sun, women sewing skins on to the frame of a newly-built kayak; all of which, in spite of the presence of a petrol pump, led us to think we were seeing primitive life in the Arctic.

From the huts a half-mile walk along the beach, the sea one side and a gravel fan sparsely covered with grass on the other, brought one to the heart of Igdlorssuit—the store, the post-office, and the petrol pump, the latter an innovation since 1961. The store, run by the Royal Greenland Trading Co., buys sealskins or any other skins and sells all that the community needs; and since the community is by now what we call civilised its needs are many—food, clothing, household goods, beer, tobacco, tools, fishing gear, boats, rifles, shotguns, ammunition, fuel for lighting, cooking, and heating, as well as for outboard engines. Thus although their main occupation has not changed in that they still live, though indirectly, by hunting and fishing, yet their way of life is very far from the self-sufficiency of their forebears when the seal or the walrus provided everything—clothing, boots, tents, kayaks, food for men and dogs, fuel for cooking and oil for lighting.

The few motor boats they have are used for fishing or for reaching places where seals may be found, with a kayak in tow or on board to be used in the final stages of the hunt. Even with modern firearms, hunting a seal calls for skill and patience; with only the harpoon of former times Nimrod himself would have been severely taxed; but in those days, of course, there were many more seals. The few seals we saw were mere fleeting glimpses of a head poked above water. A seal shot in the water in summer will probably sink anyway; hauled out on a floe they offer the hunter more chance, but even there they must be killed with one shot or they will roll into the water. In winter they are harpooned at breathing holes or stalked on the ice, both methods calling for the patience of Job and, considering the cold, a Job's fortitude. Though they are not fur seals, the skins of these ring and harp seals are valuable to the fur trade. At Igdlorssuit in 1961 I bought a dozen skins from which were made two short women's coats. The remnants provided me with only a waistcoat whereas I really wanted a pair of trousers like those worn by the oldest inhabitant of Igdlorssuit, a delightful character, shaped like a barrel, almost as broad as long, who walked about aided by a stick, a benign smile on his leathery, wrinkled face and a short cutty pipe stuck firmly in his toothless mouth.

There are some thirty brightly painted wooden houses, their immediate vicinity usually pretty squalid on account of the huskies and the absence of anti-litter laws or societies for the preservation of rural Greenland. The communal refuse dump is a long way off and everyone is expected to do their own thing. Unfortunately, what is everybody's business is nobody's business; which, by the way, was the explanation given to an enquiring visitor after the Irish "troubles" of the twenties for the fact that while a number of harmless people had been shot or had their houses burnt, the most unpopular character, against whom everybody bore a grudge, had remained unharmed. Igdlorssuit has also a church and a school and thanks to the sensible arrangement of closing the school in summer, leaving the dark, winter months for study, the place swarmed with children who had little to do beyond pestering visitors. Rather like the dogs who led a carefree, idle, well-fed life all summer only to make up for it in winter by hauling sledges on long journeys over the ice. The Igdlorssuit dogs were lucky to be fed. At Holsteinborg, a place alive with dogs and where there are no sharks to be caught to provide dog-meat, we learnt when we were there in 1962 that the dogs had to fend for themselves in summer. They managed this by scouring the harbour and the fish factory where offal, scraps of whale or reindeer meat might be picked up and oil barrels licked. They even waded about off the beach looking for small fish. There are no dogs in Godthaab where keeping them is forbidden.

The children were not always a nuisance. Simon and I, for instance, employed a volunteer crew to tow an oil-drum from the settlement to *Baroque*, getting thoroughly wet on the way when jealous rivals had to be fought off. From infancy they play about in boats and kayaks, becoming good watermen. Naturally they liked to clamber over *Baroque* if given the chance and on shore they attended our movements closely. Taking a solitary walk one afternoon, congratulating myself on having escaped detection, I was half-way up a steep, stony gully when I heard shouts from below. Half a dozen urchins were in hot pursuit. But I managed to shake them off, the gully being not much to their liking. Although the island rises to over 4,000 ft. it is not mountainous in the true sense of the word; for real mountains one must look across the 6-mile-wide channel to Upernivik Island where peaks of true Alpine character stab the sky and broad glaciers flow down to the sea. At Igdlorssuit, shut in by the hill behind, one's gaze rests constantly and inevitably upon these mountains, yet those who live there show no interest. The Greenlander seems to be immune from the love of "high places and the golden mountain tops where dwell the Spirits of the Dawn". And this is strange because they struck me as being very like Sherpas both in appearance and behaviour, the same short, sturdy figures and Mongolian features, their brown cheeks suffused with red, gay, cheerful, happy go-lucky, born gamblers, easily amused, and always ready to laugh either at us or themselves.

In the early thirties Igdlorssuit had an unusual visitor when Rockwell Kent, an American artist, built himself a house and lived there for a year in intimate contact with the natives. The house is now a ruin. *Salamina*, the interesting and entertaining book illustrated by himself, gives a true picture of life at Igdlorssuit, though even in the short span of forty years there have been changes; the houses, for instance, that then were mostly built of stones and turfs are now all of imported material. In writing about our first visit to Igdlorssuit in 1961 I felt constrained to comment upon Rockwell Kent, his book *Salamina*, and Ubekendt Island:

His descriptive powers are to be envied. He saw things

through the eyes of an artist, a man with a soul, as opposed to a man personifying, as a French writer puts it, *"le mépris de vulgarisation, du clubalpinisme, et des yahous"*. For on the first sighting of Ubekendt by this yahoo it appeared to be an uncommonly dull and barren lump whereas Rockwell Kent saw it thus: "Both by the suggestion of its name (unknown) and by its position and character—its seagirt location, the simple grandeur of its stark, snow-covered table-land and higher peaks, the dark cliff barrier that forms its eastern shore—there is the glamour of imponderable mystery about the island which dignifies it even at the gateway of a region of stupendous grandeur. Its cliffs, proclaiming inaccessibility, preclude the thought of human settlements. When, therefore, on approaching its more mountainous north-eastern end, where, just ahead, steep mountain walls rise sheer from the water's edge, the barrier ends, the shore sweeps inward in a mile-wide crescent of smooth strand and, cupped by mountains, there appears a low and gently sloping verdant foreland, jewelled with painted buildings, one's spirit, in sudden awakening to a need, exults in grateful consciousness of its fulfilment."

The crew together with odd bodies from the Manchester hut and a few Greenlanders who thrust their way in, filled the St. Andrews hut to capacity. I was disappointed to learn that both my friends were leaving that evening by boat for Umanak and thence by helicopter to the airfield at Sondre Stromfjord. The hut was well stocked with provisions of which we were invited to take what we wanted. We were also told of a climber, David Meldrum, who in a day or two would be available to accompany us to Upernivik Island. At this open roadstead we kept an anchor watch, mainly to keep an eye on drifting floes of which there were in fact few, all the bergs being well out in mid-channel. During my watch next night I took the dinghy ashore to empty it of water and met David Meldrum who was taking the air on the beach. On shore, even at midnight, there were mosquitoes about though, like the seals, they seem to have diminished in numbers over the years. David, who had climbed on Upernivik with a St. Andrews party in 1967, agreed to start on the 16th, bringing with him a Zodiac inflatable so that he could get back to Igdlorssuit on his own. At this time he was working for the Danish Geodetic Survey.

Pending our departure we put in some work on the boat and attended coffee parties in various houses. Such parties are the main social activity—Rockwell Kent has much to say about them in his book.

The clew of the mainsail needed a new cringle, a job I found difficult to do well with a strand of nylon rope; it does not hold its lay when unstranded as does tarred Italian hemp which is the proper stuff to use. We managed at last to cut away a lot more of the net still attached to the keel by swinging out the boom with enough weights suspended from it to heel the boat well over. Before we left Ilan collected the promised stores—fried onion, milk powder, honey, marmalade, Ryvita, all most welcome—and for one meal showed us how to live off the country in the manner of Stefansson's *The Friendly Arctic*. One of the local boats had brought in a small whale and in the course of my walk over the hills I had found a gigantic mushroom or some kind of fungus. Hence for supper we had mushroom soup and whale steaks.

Unless circumstances demand of them a very early start, as may happen in the Alps, mountaineers are not unduly quick off the mark. We hung about until midday before David had himself fettled up and ready to move. Towing the Zodiac we motored across to the south-west corner of Upernivik and along its south coast before turning into Pakavsa, a 2-mile-wide fjord separating Upernivik from the Qioqe peninsula. In 1961 I had had my eye on a peak on Qioqe of 7,500 ft., the highest in the region. In mountaineering, if not in life, we needs must love the highest when we see it. Before sailing, however, I learnt that the peak had been climbed by the Italian Piero Ghiglioni, aged seventy-seven, and an Italian guide, climbed, too, from sea-level in the day without any bivouac. The friend who sent me the account added: "There is hope for you yet." Piero Ghiglioni was an exceptional man who would no doubt still be climbing had he not been killed in a car accident the next year. In any case had we tried that peak Charles Marriot (on whom be peace) and I would not have succeeded. From sea-level we attempted a peak of 6,500 ft. and after eight hours, having reached about 5,500 ft., Charles had a bad attack of what I call Mountaineer's Foot, the inability to put one in front of the other. Stung by that failure we had gone to Upernivik where we had spent most of our time looking for a peak within our grasp. Had we gone there first, where there were glaciers on which one could move freely and many unclimbed peaks of great character, we might have bagged several instead of only one. As I wrote afterwards: "Instead of buzzing like elderly bees from flower to flower gathering very little honey, had we but established a high camp on Upernivik we might have drunk our fill."

Having climbed there with a very active St. Andrews party David knew well the mountains of Upernivik. He had with him, too, a map of the island and full accounts of two St. Andrews expeditions. As we motored up the fjord between towering walls of red granite, many high, slender, and apparently inapproachable spires would make their startling appearance. Whereupon I would say to David: "Well, I suppose that one has not yet been climbed", for in the eyes of a superannuated mountaineer some of the peaks looked not only as if they could not be climbed but that they were best left alone. Nothing of the sort. All had been climbed as well as several equally or even more difficult peaks on Qioqe. I doubt if there are any first ascents to be made now in that region—not that that matters, for the mountain is the same and will afford the same satisfaction when it is climbed for the five-hundredth time.

Since the war and particularly in the last fifteen years climbing standards have risen enormously, partly to the ever-increasing number of climbers, not only in England but throughout the world (the Japanese for instance), and partly owing to new equipment and new techniques. There is in some instances, too, an attitude new to mountaineering, that of death or glory, which sometimes succeeds and sometimes fails, and which in any case is foolish, because the glory is so transient. A man ought to rate his achievements only by the satisfaction they give him, for they will soon be outdone, outshone, and speedily forgotten by everyone but himself. Such climbers push their luck to the limit. In the Himalaya, for example, routes that are threatened by ice-falls to which a party may be exposed for days while it lays its fixed ropes, are cheerfully undertaken; whereas in the thirties no sober mountaineer, taught to eschew objective dangers, would have looked twice at such a route.

We hoped to anchor off the mouth of a small river, the place where the St. Andrews party had established their first base camp, and since the river, though small, is fed by melting snow and melting glaciers and must carry down a lot of silt I expected to find off its mouth water shallow enough for an anchorage. In these steep-sided fjords an anchorage is hard to find, only where glaciers and rivers debouch is there much chance. I see from the chart that the depths in Pakavsa are 500 metres, or in more seamanlike terms 270-odd fathoms. Within thirty yards or less of the rocks where the river came tumbling down we got no bottom at 10 fathoms. I gave Simon another length of line to bend on. We all make mistakes. Simon's bend was not what it should have been and at the next cast we lost our 7 lb. lead. After that I gave up and we made for the Qioqe side of the fjord where steep walls gave way to a wide valley, a glacier coming down it half-way, and a sandy beach below. Obviously a good anchorage although on the wrong side of the fjord. But we had the Zodiac.

While we were crossing the fjord Simon hastily contrived another lead out of two pieces of iron wired together. We anchored in 8 fathoms a hundred yards from the beach, a beach unsullied but for a solitary tin and the inevitable, indestructible plastic bag. As the sun sank in a cloudless sky a slender, knife-edged ridge some 5,000 ft. above cast its shadow across the glacier. The ridge led to an even more slender peak which David assured me had been climbed by a Scottish party in a climb lasting thirty-six hours, while an equally fearsome peak to the north had been climbed by an Italian party. Air transport, too, has been another contributory factor to the revolution in climbing without which mighty few peaks in Greenland would as yet have been climbed.

On 17th August, yet another flawless day, the climbing party embarked in the Zodiac and by 10 a.m. had landed at the river mouth, crossing the fjord three times as fast as we had in *Baroque*. Having moored the Zodiac, anchoring it with stones to prevent it drifting back against the rocks, we shouldered our rucksacks and set off up the left bank of the river. At the last moment Ilan had decided to come with us for a walk. In case I had to wait half the night for Simon and David I had brought a sleeping bag which I dumped there. David should have warned me about the river. At that comparatively early hour there was not much water coming down and at the mouth it was easily fordable, but as we moved up the volume of water seemed to increase rapidly. David and Simon soon forged ahead out of sight, I followed, while Ilan who had on his feet only rubbers, remained at a respectful distance behind. My chosen peak of some 4,500 ft. lay across the river a couple of miles to the south and so long as I followed the left bank it was not getting any nearer. The river, now running with intimidating force, had to be crossed and at last I found a place where although I should get wet I was not likely to be drowned. Happily the rucksack containing food and camera got across dry. A freshwater bath might have done the camera good, for after three months at sea in *Baroque* it was pretty salty. I had no ice-axe and in crossing rivers an ice-axe for taking soundings and for support, like a third leg, is invaluable. My last axe had gone down with *Seabreeze* and had not been replaced. In the original Ellesmere Island plan I had assumed that Simon and John Harradine would do the climbing and that in those comparatively unknown waters my lot would be to look after the boat.

The broad, easy slopes of the stony glacis leading to the foot of the peak provided a long, hot trudge. One could not plod along automatically with some sort of rhythm, one's mind on something else; there were too many boulders, large and small, so that every step had to be chosen. I sat down for a bite in the welcome shadow of a great rock in a thirsty land. The day was hot, the peak distant, and it did not really matter tuppence if I climbed it or not. Thus Belial, once more, with words clothed in reason's garb counselled ignoble ease. Having shed a few garments and wrung out wet trousers and socks I felt better and pressed on. A wide snow couloir led invitingly towards the summit but I found that in spite of the sun the snow remained extremely hard. Scraping a few tentative steps with my boots I soon realised that without an axe I would probably come unstuck and without an axe a slide in hard snow is difficult to stop. The first stop would probably be a violent one against some boulder where the snow ran out. But at the side of the couloir where snow met rock, progress was easy either on the rock, or on the snow, or in the gap between them.

Even the 20 ft. summit boulder which from below I had already decided to forgo—such is the caution imposed by age—offered no resistance and was soon overcome. Judging from afar whether a thing can be climbed or not is as uncertain as judging from afar the navigability or otherwise of pack-ice. The only way is to go and see. In a cairn on the summit was a cigarette tin with the four names of the St. Andrews party who had made the first ascent.

From the time they had taken one gathered they were not very fit, and it was in fact their first climb undertaken merely to gain a view-point. The solo climber, too, is at an advantage; "he travels the fastest who travels alone" with no one arguing the toss about the best route to take. This inoffensive summit, by the way, has been named "Groyling" by the St. Andrews party. So far as I know there is as yet no co-ordinating body to approve or disapprove of the names given to Greenland peaks, names now bestowed in haphazard fashion according to the whims and the nationality of the party that makes the first ascent.

From the top I could see the first obstacle, a steep snow couloir, that David and Simon would have to climb but, of course, no sign of the climbers. Even at this height yellow Icelandic poppies grew and flowered in modest profusion. Starting down the rocks of the south-east ridge I was soon tempted by a more direct route down another wide snow couloir. After a few more hours of sunshine the snow here had just the right consistency for a fast descent by making long strides with each heel dug down into the snow. With an ice-axe one could have made a fast glissade. The river had been much on my mind, for by the evening of so warm a day would be a boiling torrent. So I decided to try at the mouth where it flattened out after a steep drop and there I got across with unexpected ease. The Zodiac had drifted against the rocks in spite of our care but it had come to no harm. There was no sign of Ilan so I made a bed of heath and got into my sleeping bag, both to ward off mosquitoes and to keep warm, the sun having dropped behind the ridge. By eight o'clock I was getting worried. Unused to rough going, and ill-shod, Ilan, I felt sure, had sprained an ankle or fallen into the river, nor had I any idea which way he had gone. Half an hour later he turned up, unperturbed and seemingly untired in spite of having been wandering about since ten that morning, having much enjoyed his solitary stroll. The thought of food and drink easily persuaded us not to wait any longer and by 9 p.m. we were back on board enjoying coffee and scrambled eggs.

I sent John and Brian off to pick up the climbers. At 2 a.m. they returned complaining with some reason that they were cold and clamouring for coffee. Again I began to worry and this time with some reason. Their peak was further away than mine and altogether in a different class, but it was only a thousand feet higher and should not have taken such a young and active pair all that time. On the other hand David had climbed it before and was experienced. At 3 a.m. just as the Zodiac was about to start back again Brian saw a flare. So John went over alone and half an hour later, much to my relief, everyone was back on board. Simon was a rock climber, unused to snow and ice, and the descent of the snow couloir which by then was in bad condition had consumed a lot of time. The climb had been an eye-opener for Simon who found that mountaineering, as opposed to rock-climbing, involved toil and sweat.

David had now to get back to Igdlorssuit so having seen him off in the Zodiac we got under way down the fjord. The absence of wind gave us a chance to try out the great sweeps that Colin Putt had made, our immediate reaction to the loss of *Seabreeze*. When near the land if there is no wind, whether there is ice about or not, a boat without an engine is liable to get into trouble. If there is any wind the boat can claw off the shore, but if there is a lot of ice about as well the boat cannot sail for fear of hitting a floe. With a pair of sweeps we might have succeeded in getting *Seabreeze* close enough inshore to anchor before the gale broke and before the ice came down. The sweeps with their rowlocks fitted snugly into holes in the capping rail forward of the mast, and with two men on each we found we could move the boat at the rate of nearly a knot and turn her about easily.

CHAPTER FIFTEEN

Umanak and Homewards

Umanak, where we intended stocking up for the voyage home, is the administrative centre for this region. On the way there I had thought of visiting a new zinc-lead mine which had just become operational, but on second thoughts it seemed likely they would be too busy to welcome casual visitors. This Blank Angel mine, as it is called, is an exciting project, the ore having to be brought down 3,000 ft. by aerial cableway from the top of Black Angel mountain. This will be the only mine now active in Greenland. The cryolite mine at Arsuk which has been worked for more than half a century has been worked out; a zinc-lead mine on the east coast north of Scoresby Sound has closed down, likewise the coal mine on Disko Island. Future possibilities are a molybdenum deposit in east Greenland, an iron deposit at the bottom of God-thaab fjord, and uranium in south Greenland. No one yet knows whether there is gas or oil under the Greenland continental shelf, although the geological features are said to be favourable. The Danish Government is still pondering the implications of granting concessions which, if ever granted, would be under stringent safe-guards against pollution.

From almost anywhere in the large bay called Nordost Bugt, in which Ubekendt and Upernivik islands lie, the small island of Umanak catches the eye. Only 4 miles long and less than 2 miles wide, it comprises an uncommonly sheer rock peak that rises to 3,856 ft. Its obvious challenge, visible from 40 to 50 miles away, was first taken up by two German climbers, and it was climbed for only the second time much more recently by a St. Andrews party. As we approached it Simon and I naturally looked long and hard at this great monolith trying to discover the line of weakness in its formidable defences. The settlement crouches on the only flat bit left at the eastern end of the island. The small harbour, its entrance less than a cable wide, is sheltered from all but easterly winds. When we anchored there, putting a stern line ashore, there were only one or two small floes inside the harbour. We enjoyed the luxury of having all-night in, setting no anchor watch.

Church, school, hospital and store cluster round the harbour, leaving the private houses to perch as they can on any flat bit of rock between the harbour and the base of the mountain. On the Monday we completed our shopping, took on more diesel oil by floating a drum across the harbour, and watered from the nearest tap, rowing it off in jerrycans. That afternoon it began to blow hard from the east and small bergs began making their way into the harbour. After the Vaigat this Nordost Bugt is the most prolific source of supply for icebergs. Many large glaciers descend from the inland ice to debouch into it and many such glaciers lie not far east of Umanak; they are constantly calving and an easterly wind accelerates the drift of the bergs down the fjord to Umanak Island; and while the depth of water across the entrance does not permit the entrance of any monsters it encourages them to take the ground and pile up just outside. Many small floes were worming their way in so we moved our berth out of the direct line of entrance and set an anchor watch to fend off intruders.

Next morning, 21st August, dawned bright and sunny, the east wind still at full blast not far from gale force, and the accumulation of ice outside warned us that it was high time to go. We got our anchor and motored to the entrance where there was still room enough to pass provided one could steer the necessary devious course. *Baroque*'s whimsical ways when under power have been noticed. She sheers relentlessly to starboard, a tendency that is barely counteracted by keeping the tiller hard over. To turn to port the engine must be put in neutral. At the critical moment in the pass, as we put her in neutral to turn to port, the wind took charge and blew her off to starboard. By going full astern we narrowly missed hitting the rocks on that side. Going astern with ice floes around is particularly hazardous because there is no telling which direction she will take. The wind soon obliged her to make up her mind and as soon as she pointed towards the harbour we went back, thankful to have escaped any damage.

Once more at anchor, warding off floes and wondering what

next to do, we were presently boarded by a Greenlander who had his skiff moored close by. He began talking vehemently in a frightful mixture of Eskimo, Danish and English. The words "ice" and "come" frequently repeated were alone distinguishable but he was evidently voicing my own fears, namely that if we did not get out that day we might be there for some time, even for the winter. Accompanied by the Greenlander we rowed across to the harbour office to find someone who spoke English. A tow from the harbour tug, we learnt, would cost 100 kr. an hour for a minimum of six hours. While digesting this we saw that the tug in question, having just conducted an incoming vessel through the ice, had gone alongside *Baroque*. We took the hint, bundled the Harbourmaster into the dinghy, and rowed back to talk to the man who mattered.

The skipper of the tug understood English far better than the Harbour-master. He and his crew had been inspecting *Baroque* above and below with interest and he grasped what we wanted almost at once. He looked like an American gangster and spoke like one. Completely ignoring the Harbour-master, who was still muttering about kroners, he merely drawled out "Sure". So in with the dinghy, up anchor, and away. While still inside the harbour, ignoring or forgetting our 7 ft. 5 in. draught, he towed us right over the projecting tongue of a floe on which we ought to have grounded but just managed to slide over. With this narrow shave averted we weaved an intricate course through the clutter of ice outside and soon reached more or less open water. Casting off, waiting neither for kroners nor even cigarettes, the friendly tug sped back to Umanak. Hoisting sail, the wind as fresh as ever and right astern, we in turn sped off down the fjord, thankful to be on our way. My intention had been to return through the Vaigat, visiting either Christianshaab or Jakobshavn on the way. Both harbours are small and liable to be encumbered with bergs of which, mindful of *Baroque*'s vagaries and our recent experience, I had for the present had enough. The open waters of Davis Strait, salmon nets notwithstanding, seemed the safer course.

In Davis Strait the winds follow roughly the lie of the coast and are either from south-east or north-west, the latter predominating. We enjoyed a fine spell of northerly wind which gradually increased until on 25th August it blew hard enough for us to log nearly a hundred miles.

She should have done better than that but by now we had a good growth of grass and weed on the hull. The seeds of this growth must have been sown, as it were, during our stay in Irish waters and the cold water in which we had been for the last two months had not prevented its growing. Steering south, while the coast trended away to the south-east, we were a long way from land and near the middle of Davis Strait when we encountered the remnants of what is called the "Middle Pack", the pear-shaped field of ice that extends southwards from Baffin Bay down the middle and western half of Davis Strait. We had passed several icebergs and I had assumed that the scattered floes we now found ourselves among were merely debris from those that were breaking or disintegrating. The drop in sea temperature from 4°C. at noon to 1·5°C. at 6 p.m. should have warned me. Later that night we were still among floes which by then had become difficult to see and to avoid.

At first we hove-to but as she still forged slowly ahead we dropped the sails and lay a-hull, keeping double watches, with the engine ready to start should a floe bear down on the boat. At midnight the sea temperature fell to 0°C. and at 6 a.m. to −0·5°C., the lowest we recorded. Sea water of average salinity freezes at −1·6°C. Strangely enough, just as we hove-to that night, a great bunch of salmon net rose to the surface to be dragged on board by Brian. This must have been all that remained after our last attempt to clear it at Igdlorssuit. Even lying a-hull did not ensure a quiet night. More than once the engine had to be started and more than once a nasty thud showed that it had not been started quickly enough.

We began sailing again at dawn and by breakfast-time had got clear of the ice, the last we were to see. In bleak, dismal weather we held on southwards, making nothing to the east, as we wanted to keep well outside the north-going current that sets up the coast. So far we had done well and might have made a fast passage but for various troubles, some of them serious, that now began to plague us. The increasing play in the tiller caused some alarm. The bolts holding the iron shoe which held the tiller to the rudder stock were worn and could not be tightened. As a temporary measure we lashed it with chain.

Then on 2nd September, when we were some 200 miles west of C. Farewell, we met a gale at south-east, a direction that was worse than useless. The barometer fell to 989 mbs. and we remained hove-to for the next two days. Pumping became continuous, for the more violent squalls heeled her right over in spite of being close-reefed. Later we preferred to lie a-hull, thus keeping her more upright and lessening the drift to leeward. The snag is that instead of meeting the seas more or less bow on a boat lying a-hull is broadside on, presenting a more vulnerable target to breaking seas. There are exceptions, of course, but generally speaking a summer gale in the North Atlantic seldom lasts long enough to raise a dangerously high sea such as might be met with in the Roaring Forties.

All ills are good when attended by food—down below, digesting risotto and a pudding fit for a glass case, the whole washed down with mulled wine, one could ignore the seas outside and our inexorable drift in the wrong direction. Another bright feature was the state of the bonded store locker where we had far more than we would be allowed to take ashore. This we set about systematically to reduce. During this blow, besides a lot of pumping to do, we had some minor troubles. The hook of the topping-lift block broke allowing the boom to drop on to the doghouse with surprisingly little damage to that flimsy structure. The port side pinrail to which the peak and staysail halyards were secured came adrift and the wire life-line on that side parted. At sea one expects wear and chafe, especially if there is much bad weather, but in *Baroque*, arrange things as one might, some piece of gear always seemed to be rubbing against another.

On the evening of 5th September, the wind blowing harder as it often does when the barometer starts to rise, a small hand-mirror I used for shaving fell to the floor and broke. Sailors are traditionally superstitious. One writer whom I have consulted goes so far as to say "they are puerile in their apprehensions of omens", and then lists a few of the things that no sailor cared to meet on land much less to have on board—bare footed women with flat feet, a red-headed man with flat feet, priests, hares, pigs, lawyers and cats. The playing of cards, or worse still losing overboard a mop or bucket, presaged evil of some kind, while the ringing of a glass certainly foretold the death of a shipmate and had to be stopped instantly. Similarly whistling, umbrellas, pins, and pieces of cut hair or finger nails were taboo. Sailing on a Friday or changing a ship's name are both inadvisable. Of mirrors there is no mention. Such things would seldom be found in the fo'c'sle of a sailing ship, so it is probably only landsmen who feel concern when they break. Be that as it may, no sooner had our mirror broken than Simon came down to report the boom sprung about four feet from the after end. With something of a struggle we got the sail down and lay a-hull.

Early next morning in his watch Simon, anxious to be doing, not only got the sail off the boom but in a fit of absent-minded enthusiasm unrove the peak halyards. The boom could be repaired without doing this and meantime we could not set the mainsail, as we might have done, loose-footed without the boom. Instead we set an old canvas jib abaft the mast and with that and the staysail made some progress, the wind having at last gone north-west. Contrary winds, and the time we had lost spent hove-to roused some concern for our water supply, for we were still west of C. Farewell and a long way from home. As one small economy we cut out the midday cocoa. We had on board a big coil of $\frac{1}{8}$ in. wire that Colin Putt had provided, with a view to it being needed for the mast. There was a long scarf in the mast and some observers might have described it in the words of Mr. Chucks, the bos'un, as precarious and not very permanent. In fact it stood up manfully and gave us no concern. By revolving the boom with the reefing gear and keeping the wire under tension we put on some three feet of neat wire serving. Over this we put two of the old chain plates as splints with more wire serving over them, and on top of all a canvas coat to protect the sail when reefing.

In quieter weather Simon went aloft to hang a new block for the topping lift and to reeve the peak halyards again. As a rock-climber, accustomed to modern methods, he had with him his climbing harness. In any seaway the ratlines would shake a man off, so he was hauled up by the stays'l halyards and sitting secure in his harness, which could be clipped on anywhere, he had both hands free to work. With the peak halyards rove we set the mainsail loose-footed, the wind being fair and the work on the boom not quite finished. Sailing thus imposes a heavy strain on the clew of the sail and by the end of the day the mainsail had to come down for repair. Next day with the boom ready we were back in business. Not for long, though. By nightfall, the wind blowing hard from south-east, we were once more hove-to.

Torn sails and sprung booms, which can be repaired, caused

less concern than leaks which could not be traced, much less stopped. Drips through the deck and weeps through the topside planking did not account for the pumping we had to do and on 8th September this suddenly increased from 800 strokes a watch to over 2,000. We gave up counting. Having my young crew to get safely home I suggested making for Iceland, the only real advantage being that on a course for Iceland we could make good use of the persistent south-east winds. The distance to Reykjavik was 700 miles, only some 300 miles less than to Ireland, and since the boat would still have to be got home from there we decided to press on. Despite the double watches that the pumping necessitated and the numerous mishaps the crew remained in good heart. We kept her going that day steering north of east— the best we could do—until at midnight when the wind again increased and during my spell at the pump I found myself doing nearly a hundred strokes a minute. We took the sails down and lay a-hull.

Breaking mirrors or not, misfortune still dogged us. The wind at last packed up to leave us rolling about in thick fog, and when the sea subsided a little we started the engine in order to charge the batteries as well as to make good a few miles. The gear box began making strange noises and upon opening it up Simon found that a nut had come adrift and caused serious damage. Simon thought we might still go astern but otherwise the engine was now useless. This, of course, would be no handicap until we reached Lymington. Calms seldom last long and in mid-ocean one does better to wait for a wind. A sight that I got that evening put us just east of C. Farewell. Our latitude remained doubtful, since for six days we had had no meridian sight. A dirty night of wind and almost continuous heavy rain once more obliged us to heave-to, tearing the jib badly as we took it down. With the jib down in the cabin we had a prolonged sewing bee, three of us at work on it until well into the night and again next morning until it was finished.

By 15th September we began to think the long spell of southerly and south-easterly winds with almost incessant rain and drizzle had come to an end. The wind went round to north-west, and although it blew with some violence, we could lay the desired course. We ran on either close-reefed or sometimes under bare poles and under this rig, or lack of rig, she would make a good 3 knots, the helmsman having to work hard to keep her running straight. We were running like this when a Russian stern trawler, homeward bound, altered course to close and speak to us. "Can we do anything for you?" they hailed in very good English. "Please report us to Lloyds, London," we replied. It was expecting a lot, I suppose, for them to be on speaking terms with London. A long embarrassed silence ensued, then, "We wish you a happy voyage," and with a parting blast on the siren and much waving they resumed their course. This looked like a genuine working trawler. Two other Russian trawlers we met in the Channel off Portland, loitering with intent as the police say, looked like equally genuine spy-ships.

On the 18th, the wind for once moderate, we made a notable discovery. In quiet conditions, with no water sloshing about below, Ilan heard water coming in under the galley floor. On lifting the boards we found a regular gusher of nearly an inch bore and rising about a foot. This discovery, while alarming, was none the less welcome. By heeling her over on the other tack we reduced the fountain sufficiently for Simon to clap over it a tingle of canvas and copper sheeting held down by many screws. With one main source of leakage thus reduced we were able to revert to single watches. The play in the tiller having become much worse we shipped the iron emergency tiller. This tiller was on the short side. Short though it was the force exerted by the rudder when hove-to during a gale was sufficient to bend it into almost a half-moon. Straightening it by clobbering took some time and while this was going on we reverted to the wood tiller until it finally came away, as it were, in the helmsman's hands.

This year we had some wild weather around the time of the equinox, thus fulfilling the expectations of those who believed in equinoctial gales. Lecky, the author of *Lecky's Wrinkles*, whom I accept as an oracle in most seafaring matters, holds that there are no such things as "equinoctial gales". "Equinoctial gales," he writes, "constitute one of those prejudices of which it is wellnigh hopeless to disabuse the popular mind. Most careful observations prove conclusively that storms have no special connection with the equinoxes; yet how often does one hear a gale, occurring even three weeks one side or other of this event, referred to as an equinoctial gale." In this Lecky has the support of the Meteorological Office who should know:

The use of this expression implies that gales are more frequent (and possibly more severe) within a few days of each equinox. At any particular location in the temperate North Atlantic, the normal pattern of gale frequency runs from a minimum in summer to a maximum in winter; from the available data there do not appear to be secondary maxima around the equinoxes. There is no reason to suggest that sudden changes of weather accompany the sun's transit of the equator. As in any other season, within the temperate belt some places will enjoy settled weather at the equinox while others will suffer boisterous weather according to the positions of anticyclones and depressions at that time.

Nevertheless, in spite of Lecky and the Meteorological Office this popular myth is probably inextinguishable. It would be an interesting piece of research to discover when and why it was ever started.

After a wild night on 20th September a seam in the mainsail began to go so that had to come down, the boom coming down of its own accord with some violence when the topping lift parted. John, who went aloft sitting in Simon's harness, found the other lift badly stranded and both were sent down for splicing. These repairs were completed by next day, a day so warm and sunny that I had a bucket bath, the first and last of the voyage. On earlier voyages this had been a daily, before-breakfast ritual, observed faithfully until fairly high latitudes had been reached. On one voyage I remember one of the crew followed my example and this soon developed into an unspoken but well understood challenge as to who would give up first. In bucket baths as in more serious matters it is hard to live up to the precept of the Old English poet:

Harder should be the spirit, the heart all the bolder,
Courage the greater, as the strength grows less.

Yet another "equinoctial gale" on the 23rd obliged us to lie a-hull. By now we were approaching the area defined as "Shannon" in the Shipping Forecasts, close enough to home for us to pick them up. The gale had abated by next day when we celebrated Simon's twenty-first birthday with a three-course meal—onion soup, *moussala* (a Greek speciality of Ilan's), and peaches in rum. Replete and lethargic, with the feeling that "fate cannot touch me, I have dined today", we nevertheless had to turn out at midnight to reef.

September went out with a roar, gale succeeding gale, all from the right direction and giving us a great lift homewards, usually running with only the staysail and what we called our "comic" sail set. The much-needed trysail was lying at the sailmakers and we felt the mainsail should be nursed, not wishing to have twenty or thirty feet of seam-stitching on our hands. We passed south of the Scillies on the night of the 30th, too far off to raise the Bishop light, but on the following night we saw the loom of the Lizard, our first English light. Whereupon, by way of welcome, the wind promptly went round to the east where it remained for the following four days blowing pretty fresh. Beating against it proved unprofitable. We fetched up on the French coast east of Ile de Batz and our next board took us back to England in the vicinity of the Eddystone. For some unseamanlike reason this light escaped the notice of the man on watch and when I came on at 2 a.m. we seemed to be on the point of entering what looked like Fowey. Gybing with difficulty, for *Baroque* gybes with reluctance except accidentally, we stood out to sea and soon picked up the Eddystone light.

The east wind continued, as did our run of mishaps. In fact it blew so hard that we hove-to and let her drift rather than go on beating to small purpose. On our resuming sailing and sighting the Eddystone for the third or fourth time, the hook on the jib block broke. Once more and for the last time Simon went up to hang another block. More leaks too, under the galley floor where water was spurting up between two planks as she rolled. But by now the malice of the east wind was spent. Off Anvil Point on 6th October, the tide foul and the wind but light, Ilan and I played our last game of chess, a prolonged struggle, and by evening we were up with the Needles, carrying the last of the flood to Yarmouth where we anchored.

By sailing at dawn we expected to catch the tide and with the aid of our sweeps make our way up Lymington river. But the westerly wind died away by dawn and by the time we had crossed the Solent had come in fresh from the north. Our sweeps would be no good against that so we anchored off Lymington Spit. It was a Sunday and there were many yachts out even in October. The first yacht we hailed said he was bound for Poole and he seemed a little shaken when in reply to his query "Where from?" we answered "Greenland". Presently, however, I got a lift into Lymington where I arranged for a tow that afternoon.

So in this undignified fashion *Baroque* ended her first voyage with me, a voyage that in some respects had been troublesome. Still we had all enjoyed ourselves—which is why one goes to sea —and in spite of her troubles *Baroque* had been what is called a happy ship. Once more I could appreciate the wisdom of Conrad's old shellback Singleton. "Ships are all right, it's the men in them"; for whatever the faults of a ship, and *Baroque* had one or two, with a good crew these faults can generally be overcome. Conversely, however good the ship, with a poor crew one cannot get very far.

In climbing mountains or sailing the seas one often has to settle for less than one hoped. Instead of Ellesmere Island we had to settle for Greenland, and considering the short time we had to prepare her for a hard voyage she did well to get us there and the crew did well to get her back. In theory the skipper of a small boat should be able to do rather better than his crew anything that is required either on deck or aloft. With the handicap of age more had to be left to the crew and I was thankful to have Simon, active and competent, backed up by the others who were equally active if less competent. More important, however, is for them to have the right outlook. Activity can be instilled and competence can be acquired, but the right attitude must be ingrained—the cheerful acceptance and endurance of small privations and wearisome duties and the unquestioned belief that the success of the voyage and the care of the ship is what matters most. "This ship, the ship we serve, is the moral symbol of our life."

The Author's Boats and Voyages

MISCHIEF

Bristol Channel Pilot Cutter built 1906 by Thos. Baker, Cardiff. *Length* 45 ft., *beam* 13 ft., *draught* 7 ft. 6 in., *Thames Tonnage* 29.

1906–1919	Working pilot boat owned by William Morgan, or "Billy the Mischief".
1927	First appears in the Yacht Register and had ten different owners before being bought by H. W. Tilman in 1954.
1955–1956	Las Palmas – Montevideo – Magellan Straits – Valparaiso – Callao – Panama – Bermuda – Lymington 20,000 miles
1957–1958	Las Palmas – Bahia Blanca – Cape Town – Durban – Beira – Comoro Islands – Aldabra – Aden – Port Said – Malta – Gibraltar – Lymington 21,000 miles
1959–1960	Las Palmas – Cape Town – Iles Crozet – Kerguelen – Cape Town – St. Helena – Lymington 20,000 miles

| 1961 | West Greenland: Godthaab – Umanak fjord – Godthaab – Lymington 7,500 miles |

1961   West Greenland: Godthaab – Umanak fjord – Godthaab – Lymington   7,500 miles

1962   West Greenland: Godthaab – Evighedsfjord – Holsteinborg – Exeter Sound (Baffin Islands) – Lymington   6,500 miles

1963   Baffin Bay: Godthaab – Godhavn – Upernivik – Lancaster Sound – Bylot Islands – Pond Inlet – Godthaab – Lymington   7,000 miles
December 1963 all the frames doubled as the result of a survey which condemned her as no longer fit for long voyages

1964   East Greenland: Faeroe Islands – Reykjavik – Angmagssalik – Lymington   3,700 miles

1965   East Greenland: Reykjavik – Angmagssalik – Skjoldungen fjord – Lymington   4,000 miles

1966–1967   Las Palmas – Montevideo – Punta Arenas – South Shetland Islands – South Georgia – Montevideo – Azores – Lymington   20,400 miles

1968   Faeroe Islands – Akureyri (Iceland) – Jan Mayen. *Mischief* grounded and later abandoned in a sinking condition while under tow 30 miles east of Jan Mayen   2,500 miles

Two mountains and a cape have officially been named after *Mischief*—Mont du Mischief, by the French, on Ile de la Possession, Iles Crozet; Cap Mischief, also by the French, on Ile de Kerguelen; Mount Mischief, by the Canadian Survey Department, Exeter Sound, Baffin Island near Mount Raleigh.

SEABREEZE

Bristol Channel Pilot Cutter built 1899 by J. Bowden, Porthleven. *Length* 49 ft., *beam* 14 ft. 4 in., *draught* 7 ft. 6 in., *Thames Tonnage* 33.

1969	Seydisfjord (Iceland) – East Greenland coast – Lymington	3,400 miles
1970	West Greenland: Faeringehavn – Ivigtut – Juliane-haab – Prins-Christian Sund – Lymington	4,900 miles
1971	Reykjavik – Isafjord – off Scoresby Sound – Ang-magssalik – Sehestedshjord – Lymington	5,000 miles
1972	Reykjavik – Isafjord – off Scoresby Sound. *Seabreeze* grounded and foundered on the way home south of Angmagssalik	3,000 miles

BAROQUE

Bristol Channel Pilot Cutter built 1902 by J. Hambly, Cardiff. *Length* 50 ft., *beam* 13 ft. 6 in., *draught* 7 ft. 6 in., *Thames Tonnage* 32.

1973	Cork – Bantry Bay – Godthaab – Umanak fjord – Lymington	5,700 miles
1974	Left Lymington bound for Spitsbergen	

Baffin Island
Nugssuaq
Disko I.
Jakobshavn
Davis Strait
Holsteinborg
GREENLAND
Godthaab
Faeringehavn
Sermilik
C.Dan
Angmagssalik
Denm
Frederikshaab
Sehesteds Fjord
Julianehaab
Cape Farewell
50°W
40°
30°